THE 19TH HOLE

THE 19TH HOLE

FAVORITE GOLF STORIES

Carol Mann

LONGMEADOW PRESS

Copyright © 1992 by Carol Mann

Published by Longmeadow Press, 201 High Ridge Road, Stamford,
CT 06904. All rights reserved. No part of this book may be
reproduced or utilized in any form or by any means, electronic or
mechanical, including photocopying, recording or by any information
storage and retrieval system, without permission in writing from the
Publisher.

Library of Congress Cataloging-in-Publication Data
The 19th hole : favorite golf stories / Carol Mann. — 1st ed.
    p. cm.
  ISBN 0-681-41455-3
  1. Golf—Anecdotes. I. Mann, Carol. II. Title:
Ninteenth hole.
GV967.A18 1992
796.352—dc20   92-10801
                            CIP

Cover design by Mike Stromberg
Interior design by Allan Mogel
ISBN: 0-681-41455-3
Printed in the United States
First Edition
0 9 8 7 6 5 4 3 2 1

To my father,
who taught me about
sportsmanship and honor.

CONTENTS

CONTENTS

INTRODUCTION

For many years I have avoided writing a book. I believed it was something people did at the end of something, like certain achievements, or near death, when perhaps real enlightenment might occur.

Since I have felt neither the approach of death nor the diminishment of my passion for golf and the people who play it, this book is a celebration of my mid-passage in golf. It is less about what I know and more about whom I know.

In 42 years of playing golf, I have swapped stories with great players, caddies, renowned athletes, entertainers, businesspeople, politicians, clubhouse attendants, friends, relatives—so many people. Golf can be a great leveler. Everyone who walks out onto a course, regardless of how famous he is or how great a player she is, will bring back to the 19th hole (where the drinks are served) some story of bad luck, good luck, awfulness of a shot, brain glitches, nerve twitters, stupid judgment, puffed-up confidence, or some strange occurrence that seems to bring us all together. Sometimes there are even stories of golf gone well—making a hole-in-one, sinking a rollercoaster putt, or winning a match we weren't supposed to. These stories get repeated even more often.

I have had the opportunity to meet and befriend a lot of terrific people. And I've heard some terrific golf stories. The idea for this book came from my good friend and associate Ted Royal. It seemed so simple and such a natural idea for me to ask my friends and compatriots to contribute their favorite golf stories for a book. I asked Jack Lemmon first. Charles "Sparky" Schulz was next. Then Bob Hope, and I was off and running. Not all the people I asked contributed. Mike Schmidt didn't think anything funny had ever happened to him while playing; Chris Evert just had a difficult pregnancy and didn't want to upset the baby with memories of her golf exploits.

Since I have been a professional golfer for more than half my life, I thought I'd start things off with one of my own favorite stories, one that you'll see helped propel me even further into a golf career.

I was lucky. When my father, Rip, was transfered to Chicago, he and my mother, Ann, decided they needed a great country club for themselves and their brood, four younger brothers and I, to have fun in the summertime. They joined Olympia Fields Country Club, which had been the site of many historic championships in the past.

When I was 14 years old, one of the most important women's amateur events was played on the South Course, the Women's Western Amateur Championship. I had a handicap of 28, too high to enter the tournament. Somehow, at the last minute, the committee decided to let me play. I was excited, but scared. The other young women competitors, a little older than I, had so much poise and confidence. And they dressed very well. I didn't have any clothes that looked really attractive. I went to a private girls' school and wore a uniform. My wardrobe was also limited by my height. Already I was close to six feet tall. I was gawky and quite self-conscious.

In the qualifying round I shot 114 to be placed in the fifth and last flight. On the second day, I lost my match, so I was put into the fifth flight consolation matches. This is about as low as any competitor can go, but I didn't know that at that time. All I knew was I got to play again the next day. I won that match, the next, and the next. I was still in it, and thrilled!

The prizes for the tournament and flight winners were carefully and beautifully displayed in the immense lobby of the club. The evening before my final match, I sneaked a peek at the winner and runner-up prizes for all flights, including my exciting consolation flight. The trophies were real silver. They sparkled. One of those was to be mine. I didn't care which, the winner or runner-up. I was ready to cherish either.

Since I was to play early, I went to bed early, but I was so excited it was tough going to sleep. My opponent and I teed off in the morning dew. The championship match went off about three hours later. When we came around to the long, par-five 18th hole, I was one down. I was over the green in four shots, on a very difficult lie—a downslope with fluffy grass all around my ball. My opponent was on the green in four strokes, about 40 feet away. In the meantime, what seemed like a thousand people were following the big final match between two very good players, Pat Lesser (later, after marriage, Pat Harbottle) and Wiffi Smith. The gallery was moving from the seventh green to the eighth tee. In between sat the eighteenth green, where I was about to play my chip shot. There was lots of shushing for the spectators to be quiet. Many members of Olympia Fields were watching and later I was told what happened next made them very proud of their only representative in the tournament.

I stole a quick glance at the crowd. I was certain they expected me to dump the ball in the little trap between my ball and the edge of the green. Well, I fooled everyone, including myself: I chipped in! The people went wild with applause. That was my first taste of playing in front of people. I was surprised at how much fun it was to have them watching me. That was my christening at what my father called "being a ham."

I won the hole, so off we went to the 19th hole (which, in this case, was the first hole, played a second time) to decide the match. No one followed us down that first fairway, so when I won it felt a bit anticlimactic. Still, as the fifth-flight consolation winner, I was presented with the most beautiful silver bowl, a lion head on each side. I slept with it that night and kept hearing the cheers and applause. That lovely bowl adorns my trophy room even today.

It's a long way from that 19th hole to this one, but not quite as long as since the first use of the term. As you probably know, the term means the bar of a golf club or course—where the best stories are swapped. The earliest-known written use of the word dates to 1915, when the prolific golf course architect and writer, A. W. Tillinghast, included it in his book *Cobble Valley Golf Yarns.* "Tillie" wrote, "We called Jim Donaldson the 'Sage' at Cobble Valley, because in the kingdom of the Nineteenth Hole he was 'Philosopher Extraordinary and Authority Unquestioned.'"

A few years later, in 1919, Robert K. Risk published "The Golfaiyat of Dufar Hyyam." *Songs of the Links* has the verse:

> "And softly by the Nineteenth Hole reclined
> Make Game of that which maketh Game of thee."

Today, over 25,000,000 people play golf in the United States alone. The fastest-growing segment of this population is women.

My fondest hope is that all the new players have the chance to learn and appreciate the style and grace of the game which has so enriched my life and the lives of all of the amateurs, professionals, men and women who have competed in the sport up to now.

I have experienced so many dimensions of golf: winning and losing, teaching and coaching, writing articles, commentating on the play of men and women for television and radio, serving as president of the LPGA and on its Board of Directors, etc. And I've enjoyed every single facet. I hope you'll have your own favorite moments, playing, reading this book, and telling your own stories the next time you're at the 19th hole.

ACKNOWLEDGMENTS

My appreciation to: Daniel Bial, Senior Editor of Longmeadow Press, who helped bring this bouillabaisse to the
table; Ted Royal, The Quaestus Group, who had the vision
to link me with this book idea and for his steady hand
throughout completion; Bob Hoffsis, Robert Hoffsis Enterprises, for his quiet insight, golf story guidance, and support;
Ray Volpe, Sports Marketing International, for his belief in
the project; Frank Weimann, The Literary Group, for his
dogged selling of the idea; Alison Frost, research manager,
for her outstanding skills, humor, patience and ideas which
contributed to momentum, organization, and success; Allan
Mogel for his artful contributions with the potpourri of photo-
graphs; Andy Gibson, Bill Strasbaugh, the late Jim Scott, the
late Irv Schloss, Manuel de la Torre, all teachers who contributed to my success as a golfer; Dr. Fran Pirozzolo, Chief,
Neuropsychology at Baylor College of Medicine; Marjorie
Gallun, Carol Mann, Inc.; William Royal, TRI; Rolland

ACKNOWLEDGMENTS

Todd, Masterful Coaching; Deborah Larkin, Lyn St. James, Jenifer Miller, Women's Sports Foundation; Edward Dey in Paris; Stephen Axthelm and other members of the Axthelm family; the late Norman Cousins; Sandi Higgs, LPGA; Sid Wilson, PGA Tour; Jeff McBride, PGA Tour photographer; "Doc" Giffin, Arnold Palmer Enterprises; Bev Norwood, International Management Group; Bob Allen, Chairman, AT&T, Jim Merrigan, AT&T; Ivy McLemore, Sports Editor, *Houston Post;* Nancy Stulack, Andrew Mutch, Diane Becker, Joan Anfinsen, Bob Somers, all from the United States Golf Association; Gina Roccanova, assistant to Senator Bill Bradley; Dave Thomas, Wendy's International; George Lewis' Golfiana and Susan Lewis; Russell Neel, Jr.; all those who contributed and their remarkable assistants; those who did, but didn't make the final cut, and those who were invited, but unable to make it this time.

Amy Alcott

COUNTRY CLUB SANDWICHES

This story happened on one of my first years on the Tour in the mid-1970s. We were playing at Wykagyl Country Club near New York City, at the Golden Lights LPGA Classic. I didn't know where to stay when I came into New York.

I had fared well my first and second years on tour and was feeling real good about myself. Some of the bigger names on tour were staying at the Westchester Country Club. I went over there and looked at it. They had this huge polo field-like driving range and it was just a gorgeous place. It was a little too expensive for my pocketbook, but I thought, "What the hell."

I checked into the country club. Pro-am day of the tournament was on Wednesday and I teamed with a gentleman who was the President or the Vice-President of Hebrew National. He asked me where I was staying and I told him. He said, "Wow, that's a pretty nice spot. Do you have a refrigerator there?" I told him I didn't. But the next day, at the golf course, he sent over three kosher chickens, two pastramis, a couple pounds of corned beef, and five kosher Hebrew National salamis and hot dogs. So I sat there with this huge box of food thinking, "This is great. I love golf. But what the hell am I going to do with all this food?"

I took the box back to the country club. The front desk there was basically deceased—it was such a quiet, eccentric old club with a few hotel rooms in its beautiful old building. As I strolled passed it, I walked up to the rickety elevator, pushed the button, and glanced next to me. The tournament roses and trophies were in a refrigerated cabinet in the foyer of the country club entrance. You could practically see the light go on over my head. As soon as I could, I had the chef slice up all the pastrami, corned beef, turkey and chicken. Then I went into Rye, New York, and bought corn rye bread, mustard, and coleslaw. I put everything into a huge box and stashed them inside the trophy case beside the elevator. Over the next few nights, whenever I got hungry, I trekked downstairs to the lobby in my robe and made myself a sandwich.

During the course of the week, I had two parties. Caddies came over, hotel guests, and it seemed like just about everybody spent the week eating out of a big, brown box on the floor of the Westchester Country Club lobby.

I look back now at what an entrepreneur I was, being able to keep this box covered up with a blanket, right in the middle of the lobby with people going by. Nobody at the club ever knew what was going on.

Amy Alcott has won 29 events on the LPGA tour, including the U.S. Open of 1980 and four other major titles, including a record three Dinah Shore Championships. She is on the verge of gaining entry into the LPGA Hall of Fame. Amy is often sought after by the media for her observations. Her charitable events include a fundraising event for Multiple Sclerosis and a fully-endowed scholarship program for women's golf at UCLA.

Dave Anderson

PLAYING WITH CURTIS STRANGE

David Spindel

Not every golf story occurs on a golf course. As a sports columnist for *The New York Times,* my favorite developed during the 1976 Masters in the interview area of the Augusta National media center.

Out on the back nine Raymond Floyd was completing his runaway victory that year when Curtis Strange finished as the low amateur. In memory of Bobby Jones, the Masters always makes a fuss about its low amateur. Strange, then a 21-year-old Wake Forest student, was brought to the stage of the interview area.

Instead of one of the usual Augusta National members conducting the interview, a portly white-haired member in a green jacket sat in the other chair up on the stage behind two microphones.

"Gentlemen," the green jacket drawled, "we have our low amateur, Cu'tis Strange, here in the interview room. Any of you gentlemen have a question for Cu'tis, you go right ahead."

But not many sportswriters had a question. To be truthful, not many cared about the low amateur. They were too busy staring at Floyd's progress on the television sets hanging from the ceiling. After two or three questions from Virginia writers representing Strange's hometown area, the silence frustrated the white-haired green jacket.

"Cu'tis," he announced in his drawl, "I got a question for you."

Strange turned in surprise. Committeemen usually don't ask questions.

"Cu'tis," the green jacket said, "as a young man attendin' Wake Forest on an Ahnuld Pawmer scholarship, it musta been a great thrill for you to play here with Ahnuld at Augusta National in the first round of the Mastuhs golf tournament. What a thrill that must've been, playin' with Ahnuld. How'd that feel, playin' with Ahnuld?"

"Well, sir," Strange said politely, "I didn't play with Arnold."

"That's right, you played with Jack," the green jacket said. "What a great thrill that must've been, playing with Jack Nicklaus at Augusta National in the first round of the Mastuhs golf tournament. How'd that feel, playin' with Jack?"

"Well, sir," Strange said, "I didn't play with Jack either."

"You didn't play with Ahnuld, you didn't play with Jack," sputtered the green jacket, annoyed and embarrassed. "Who'd you play with?"

"I played," Strange said, "with Gay Brewer."

In the laughter from the assembled sportswriters, the green jacket's face reddened. Then a voice from a corner of the interview area called, "How'd it feel playing with Gay Brewer?"

Just as that green-jacketed committeeman had never been sighted in the interview area before, he hasn't been sighted there since.

Dave Anderson is a Pulitzer Prize-winning sports columnist for *The New York Times* and a great friend of golf.

Mario Andretti
A DRIVER DRIVES

My first experience with golf was back in 1966. In Indianapolis, there is the famous driver's golf tournament, with great prizes, held after all the qualifying for the Indy 500 is over. The 18-hole course was right next to the speedway. The golf pro, Mike Sullivan, who's no longer with us, was a great friend of mine through Al Dean, the guy for whom I was driving. He was very intense, and had all these intentions to make a great golfer out of me. He even got me the most

7

beautiful set of clubs from MacGregor, with a very expensive bag—all alligator skin. I found myself intimidated by it—and especially in those days, I wasn't used to being intimidated by too many things. The bag was worth a lot more than my game.

My son Michael has been golfing for a few years and he takes it very seriously. About two years ago he started talking to me about my taking up the game again and going out with him. He bought me a set of really nice clubs for my birthday, so I had to go. My first outing with these clubs was in Phoenix, Arizona. I was playing with my old-style intensity, and on one hole my ball lay behind a cactus and a bush. I didn't have much of a shot, but I just didn't want to take a drop. I had probably 60 feet to the fringe and I gave it all I had.

I followed the flight of the ball very closely, and it landed right next to the green. I was feeling quite proud of myself until Michael came up behind me and said, "Dad, was it really worth that?"

What I hadn't especially noticed was that I hit the bush. The shaft of the club didn't bend from the collision because it was a carbon graphite shaft. It just all came apart. It frayed. I've never seen anything like it. A $120 club bit the dust.

I've learned to like golf, but that was an expensive lesson for a guy whose good game is around 100–102 strokes.

Mario Andretti, has won the Indianapolis 500 four times, and has 51 Indy Car victories. In 1978 he won the Formula One World Championship, and in 1986 the Indy Car "Triple Crown." In addition, he has won the Daytona 500, the Sebring 12-hour endurance race, the USAC National Dirt Track Championship and International Race of Champions title. He is one of only two men to win Driver of the Year honors three times.

Patty Berg
LEARNING THE HARD WAY

When I was a youngster growing up in Minneapolis I lived at 5001 Kofax Avenue South. About seven doors down from me lived a fellow by the name of Charles "Bud" Wilkinson—and what a great athlete he was. He went on to quarterback at the University of Minnesota and then to serve as coach of the Oklahoma University Sooners who won a record 47 games in a row. He also would serve as the head coach of the football Saint Louis Cardinals. He was three or four years older than I was, and the leader of our group; as youngsters, we'd play whatever game he played. If he played baseball, we played baseball. If he played football, we played football. If he played hockey, we played hockey.

Also on our block were a lot of kids who were good athletes. Our football team was known as the 50th Street Tigers. Bud was the captain, guard and coach. I was the quarterback because I was the only one who could remember the signal. We only had one signal: 22. I called "22" and everybody ran whichever way they wanted.

We didn't have any tricky plays or special formations, we just used the single wing—I was the only one back there. We didn't have any tight ends, just a lot of loose ends. We never lost a game, just teeth. Bud finally told me to quit football (after I'd donated several teeth of my own to the game) because I was too slow, too short, and there was no future for me in football.

My parents were happy as I tore all my clothes, skinned my knees, arms, hands, and frequently sported a black eye. So, I took up competitive speed ice skating. I did fairly well at that and won quite a few medals in my class. Then, during an intermediate competition, one of the other girls was already around the rink before I even got started. I figured at that moment that I'd better find something else.

One day I saw my dad's clubs in the garage, so I took one of them out and started to swing. I did that for several days. My dad could not figure out who was making all the divots in his beautiful backyard. Finally, one day he caught me swinging and said, "How would you like to get a golf ball in front of that swing?" I said, "That would be great!" And that's how I got into golf.

I've been asked many times what I consider my most satisfying moment in golf. It's really difficult for me to pick a single moment, a single occasion, a single tournament, or a single shot in my career that stands above the rest because I feel my entire life is and has been golf. I feel that I have been very fortunate in having it that way. From a playing stand-point, my most satisfying moment was in 1934.

In 1933, at age 14, I had played in my first Minneapolis City Championship. I remember on Sunday night, before qualifying on Monday, I went into the living room with my golf bag. I had a towel here and a towel there on my bag, and I said to my dad, "How do I look?" He said, "Are you going to go swimming or are you going to play in a golf tournament?"

The next day I qualified with 122 strokes. Actually, I was very lucky to have shot only 122. On one hole I chipped in, kind of like a beeline shot. Then on another hole, I was in the bunker and I shanked the ball. It grazed the top of the bunker, hit the flag, and jiggled down into the cup. So, you can see that 122 was more like 132. I was really very, very lucky because I hit a lot of bad slices that were headed out of bounds—but hit something and stayed in.

Another lady shot 121, and we were placed in the last flight—the tenth flight—just the two of us. She proceeded to beat me like a drum.

I remember she won the first hole of our match. It was a par four. I had a seven and she had a six. I hit it all over the place.

I lost the second hole, too. Then I said to my caddy, "How do you like my game?" He said, "It's okay, but I still prefer golf."

On the third hole she hit it into the water and my caddy said, "We've got her now." So I hit mine into the water. Then she hit hers into the water again. (This was a par three.) Then I hit into the water. Then she shanked her ball, but chipped across on the green. My caddy said, "She's lucky." I said, "I can't help that. She's on the green." Then I went into the water and finally gave it to her. I was three down then. I asked my caddy, "What am I doing wrong?" He said, "I think you need a lesson."

I lost the fourth hole because I sliced my drive. My caddy said to me, "You know, this bag is getting heavy." On the fifth hole I said to my caddy, "I'm not playing my usual game today. I've played better." He said, "What game do you usually play?" I lost the fifth hole too, because I jumped all over the fairway. I just couldn't figure out what caused all of these things. I must have had an eight for that hole. On the sixth hole my play was even more miserable.

Now on the seventh hole, my opponent hit two balls out of bounds. My caddy raced over to me and said, "We surely have her on this hole." Well, I hit my drive right down the middle of the fairway. But my second shot found the lake to the left. The pro then came down and said, "All the other ladies have played their match, had their lunch, and gone home." And I said, "Well, we've had a lot of trouble."

My caddy said, "That's the understatement of the year."

I said to the pro, "I've run out of golf balls—they're all in the water." I had to borrow a couple of golf balls from my opponent. I just could not maneuver the water.

I was then seven down and my caddy said to me, "You know. We are in deep, deep trouble. We have to get going." I said, "You're right. But I don't know what I'm doing wrong." The caddy didn't know what to tell me then.

On the eighth hole I hit my best drive of the day. I could hit them long, but they just went all over the place. This was my best one—straight and trouble-free. But I managed to find trouble anyway as there was a deep trap just short of the green—kind of a fairway bunker. I spent some time in there—enough time to lose the hole. So that made it eight down.

It looked as if I might tie the hole on the ninth. All I had to do was hole out a five-foot putt. I missed it. So with that, we went on to the tenth, to the eleventh. . . .

I lost every hole. I congratulated my opponent and she said, "You didn't play very well." My caddy said, "That's all right. You just didn't have any luck today." I admitted I needed more than luck. Then he said, "You know, you hit that ball in places where even Sam Snead couldn't hit it out."

As I walked back to the clubhouse, all I could think about was next year's Minneapolis City Championship. I decided right then that I was going to devote the next 365 days to improving my golf game. I went home and told my dad how miserably I played. He asked if I did anything right and I said, "Yeah, I paid the caddy."

So I practiced all day and went to the driving range at night. I thought if I worked every day, and if I had the will to win, and the desire, drive, determination and self-control, and the patience, and the will to strive for perfection and conquer all the pitfalls, and if I had the spirit and faith and enthusiasm and a winning attitude with positive thoughts, then maybe I could do better in 365 days.

Well, winning the Minneapolis City Championship at the age of 15 was the turning point of my whole career. I don't think I would be in golf today if I hadn't improved that much. I didn't believe that I would win in 1934, but I hoped I might move up a flight or two, and not shoot 122 and be defeated on every hole. But when I went on to win after dedicating 365 days to a goal, I really started to dream. I started saying to myself, "After winning the Minneapolis City Championship, maybe I could play in a Minnesota League and in the Ladies State Championship. Maybe I could play in some major golf amateur championships. And maybe someday I could have golf as my livelihood."

And this is the way it turned out. I'll never forget those 365 long days from 1933 to 1934. That's a long time to work on just one endeavour after such a shaky start.

Patty Berg is one of the most durable athletes of all time. Even after cancer recovery, hip replacement, and knee and back surgeries, she still continues to delight and entertain audiences all over the country with her infectious humor and love for golf. Patty won 57 tournaments and is in the LPGA, PGA, World Golf, Women's Sport Foundation, Minnesota, and Florida Halls of Fame. She is one of the 100 Heroes of American Golf.

Tommy Bolt
IT'S THE CLUB'S FAULT

Some people remember me for my flinging clubs or breaking them more than anything else. But often my anger was just a show. Fans would be disappointed if I didn't give them a show. They'd shout at me, "Throw it! Throw it!" I paid the price for everybody's temper.

When Arnold Palmer first started on the tour he traveled with me. I have never known a more temperamental man than Arnold Palmer. He threw clubs, cursed golf courses. . . . You wouldn't believe all that he did.

After a practice round one time, he got mad and threw his club backward where we'd already been. I then turned to him and said, "Arnold, never throw the club where you've already been. Throw it where you're going so you

15

can pick it up along the way." Arnie's wife, Winnie, was always having to go back and pick his clubs up. That's the truth.

Another golfer who let his anger show was Ky Lafoon. He chewed tobacco and would spit on his ball if it didn't go into the hole.

Ivan Gantz used to step on his driver. When he'd miss a drive, he'd stomp the heel of his right foot on the top of the driver and tear a hole in it. By the end of the tournament it looked like he'd turned a bunch of termites loose in his bag.

All good golfers have to learn how to convert the anger and use it positively. It gave me the incentive and the desire to win.

When you're winning, everybody's your friend. You cannot win and have anything but golf on your mind. You've got to be at peace with yourself to win.

My favorite story happened about 30 years ago—and Bob Hope won't let me forget it. I was playing in the old Crosby tournament at Pebble Beach. It had been a rough day, and I had treated my clubs as roughly as they treated me. At the sixteenth hole, I hit my drive down the fairway. My caddy and I looked across the ravine over to the green and I said, "Son, how far is it into the green and the hole over there?" He said, "Mr. Bolt, it's about 135 yards." I told him to give me my seven-iron. He said, "Mr. Bolt, it's either a three-iron or a three-wood. Those are the only two clubs you've got left."

Tommy Bolt is known also for his incredibly athletic and fluid golf swing which produced 11 PGA tour victories including the U.S. Open in 1958. As a senior player, Tommy has won 12 unofficial titles throughout the world.

Bill Bradley
THE FLYING GOLF CLUB

U.S. Senate Photo Studio

My mother is a really big golfer. She used to do her best to keep me in practice. We'd play once a year when I went home for Christmas.

As a Senator, I play once a year at an annual meeting of Japanese and American legislators. Each year we set aside three hours to get together on the golf course, rain or shine.

One year, when it came time to play, torrents of rain were pouring down and the wind was whipping fiercely. Nevertheless, we sallied forth.

17

As I went to hit the ball, my club went with a sudden gust of wind: it flew out of my hands, over the cliff, and into the ocean.

Bill Bradley captained the U.S. basketball team that won the gold medal at the 1964 Olympics; he then starred at forward for the New York Knicks. The Knicks won two NBA championships in his 10 years with the team. Senator Bradley was the youngest member of the U.S. Senate when he arrived in 1979. He is now the senior Senator from New Jersey.

Art Buchwald

ONCE A CADDY . . .

Bill O'Leary, *Los Angeles Times*

The reason that I don't play golf is because I was a caddy when I was 13 years old. I worked on weekends and was assigned the job of carrying the bags of women golfers—two bags for each woman. Please don't think that I am sexist, but they didn't play too fast. In those days, unlike now, women preferred to talk rather than swing.

THE 19TH HOLE

It wasn't the weight of the bags that made me abandon the game, it was the fact that the women never gave up a ball that was lost somewhere in the trees and thicket and down through the poison ivy. It was during one of these searches that I vowed to the Lord above that if I ever earned enough money, I would never set foot on a course again.

All my friends are out playing golf these days. It doesn't bother me because while they play golf, I can get all the free parking in town that I want.

Art Buchwald is the Pulitzer Prize-winning humorist and best-selling author.

19
William C. Campbell
SPORTSMANSHIP PLUS EXCELLENT GOLF

One of my most vivid memories of some two decades of traveling to Pinehurst, North Carolina, for the North and South Amateur was watching the 1951 championship match between the charismatic Billy Joe Patton of Morganton, North Carolina, and his attractive, fun-loving young friend, Hobart Manley, of Savannah, Georgia. Both long hitters had attracted a crowd which grew as their match progressed, and it turned into an intense and memorable golfing experience for all of us onlookers—not to mention the finalists themselves.

On the par-five eighth hole of the afternoon round—the 26th of the match—Manley drove far left into some scrub pine trees. After advancing his ball, he emerged from the pines and shouted to Patton that he had incurred a penalty stroke and thus lay three. Rather than going for the green, Patton then played a conservative second shot short of the green.

When Manley returned to the fairway, the referee, native Scot "Willie" Wilson, asked him about the penalty. Hobart replied that his ball had been moved slightly by something he had stepped on in the underbrush while entering the area with his hands held high. Mr. Wilson ruled that no violation had occurred, and so advised Patton. When the result was a halve in fives, Hobart told Billy Joe how badly he felt about the rules incident. Billy Joe's quick response was, "Get me a Coke (at the halfway house behind the green) and we'll call it even."

But Hobart still felt badly and brooded until the long tenth hole, which he obviously contrived to butcher by aiming his drive into the right woods, then left and right, before conceding the hole. On the eleventh tee the match resumed its high level of play, stroke for stroke, as tension mounted.

Patton stood two-up on the fourteenth tee and proceeded to play those five great finishing holes in one stroke under par—scoring par-four, par-three, birdie-four, bogey-four, and birdie-three—only to lose one down to Manley's five straight threes, which were four strokes under par: birdie, par, eagle, par, birdie. That both players at the end of a long competitive week were under such intense pressure made both their performances no less than remarkable.

Just watching the drama unfold made my heart pound and left me limp. And I wasn't alone, for it was apparent at the presentation ceremony that both winner and runner-up were emotionally spent. Indeed, there were few dry eyes in the audience, for we all seemed to realize that we had been privileged to experience amateur golf at its very best in both performance and sportsmanship. Now, 40 years later, I still regard the 1951 North and South final as one of golf's greatest days.

In later years Patton would become a folk hero to play-for-fun golfers, as he burst on the world scene in the 1954 Masters and went on to confirm his talents in several subsequent Masters and U. S. Opens and on several Walker Cup teams. He would also win three North and South Amateurs. One of them, in 1962, he won after beating Manley in a rematch, 7 and 6.

Manley had the greatest natural ability I have seen in a half-century of amateur golf. The game probably came too easily to him, for he missed the discipline needed for even gifted athletes to reach and sustain their full potential. But on that fine April Sunday in Pinehurst, he achieved such heights that anything else could well have been anticlimactic.

Of course, Patton was the other half of that story. Together they were beautiful.

William C. Campbell won the North and South Amateur four times between 1950 and 1967. He has served as President of the United States Golf Association and Captain of the Royal and Ancient Golf Club of St. Andrews, Scotland.

JoAnne Carner

DRIVING A TRAILER

AP Photos

Perhaps my most memorable win came at the World Championship in Cleveland at Shaker Heights, Ohio, because that put me in the LPGA Hall of Fame. Unfortunately I had agreed to go and play the following weekend in the Popcorn Open in Orville Redenbacher country. I had to leave right after play, so my husband Don and I never really got to celebrate the win.

I've always worked with Don. Even though I've taken

lessons from Sam Snead and Gardner Dickinson, Don helped me with my golf swing more than anybody. We were forever working to get ready for the next tournament or to stay sharp for the short game. He never let me totally rest. I could never get careless with my golf game. If I'd shoot a good round he would usually have a comment on how I could have even played better. He was forever thinking of next week's tournament and trying to keep me sharp. He's a nervous wreck when he watches anyway.

I was playing the Peter Jackson in St. George, New Brunswick, which is really the Ladies Canadian Open, and I was several shots behind. I shot a 64 the last day to come from behind and win. When I came off the green, Don came out to kiss me and congratulate me and he said, "You know you're standing hooked." And with a chuckle I said, "Can't you at least let me celebrate my win?"

We travelled in a travel trailer from the start of my pro career. We just decided that that was going to be the way to go. We had met a friend, Dick Hart from Chicago, and he traveled the men's tour that way. He found it to be enjoyable, reliable, relaxing and said that that was the way to go. We started it that way and actually enjoyed it. I played my best golf when I was in the travel trailer. It's a little more relaxing and I you don't overwork. I think when you stay in a motel you can start to climb walls and tend to spend too much time at the golf course.

We always parked the trailer in a nice area, usually on a lake or a river. And consequently we'd be able to relax and forget golf a little bit. We had invited friends over and cooked out. It was good for Don, too. He always had something to do by puttering around and fixing something on the trailer. I played golf and I cooked, although Don's a better cook, and he did the dirty stuff. For 13 years we drove from one tournament to the next. Although it got complicated when either of us would fly off on vacation or as I kept doing better and better, I'd have to do things on Mondays. Don and I would get separated and he'd have to drive it by himself, which eventually became a little too difficult.

So, back to the Popcorn Open. On the ninth hole turn I received a phone call from the "Today Show" telling me I had been named Athlete of the Week. They wanted me to come on their show. I told them I had made plans to go to High Point, North Carolina for the next regular tournament. They said they would call me back after making television arrangements out of there. They called 30 minutes later and said they couldn't film there because of a strike that was going on with the local television station. A network hook up wasn't possible so they said I'd have to go to New York and do the broadcast live on the show. They even volunteered to fly me back out, but I told them no because Don and I are never separated for more than one day, and hardly ever separated to begin with. I said, "I can't fly to New York." And they replied, "But you've got to fly to New York." And I said, "No, I don't. I want to spend time with my husband." I felt that was very important and I wanted to be with him. The woman on the phone was just flabbergasted that I wouldn't come. I told her again that if she were to make arrangements in High Point I'd be there.

I flew into High Point around midnight. Don and I sat in the trailer toasting my win. I woke up and played a breakfast practice round. Wednesday I played the pro-am and was playing with an executive from Henredon Furniture Company. He said that he'd been all excited to hear that I was going to be on the "Today Show" from the tournament but was disappointed not to have seen me. I told him why I hadn't gone to New York. "By the way, I asked. "Did I win Athlete of the Week?" He said, "No." I asked who won and he said, "a horse." And not only that, the horse had finished third. So Athlete of the Week was one of those great awards that I almost won.

JoAnne Carner established herself as a great amateur player by winning the USGA Girls' Junior, five U.S. Women's Amateur championships and representing the United States on four Curtis Cup teams before she was 30 years old. In 1969, JoAnne became the last amateur to win an LPGA tournament. Since turning pro in 1970, JoAnne has won two U.S. Opens and a total of 40 more LPGA events. She is a member of the LPGA, Women's Sports Foundation and World Golf Halls of Fame, and was elected one of the 100 Heroes of American Golf.

Susan Clark

LOOK THE PART

Babe Didrikson Zaharias is still remembered as quite the feminist, though the word probably never crossed her lips. She's a true heroine—even for people who have never picked up a golf club. When somebody is so talented and reaches out for something beyond themselves it makes them memorable.

When I was spending five hours a day, five days a week— what seems to be a hundred years ago—preparing for the television movie *Babe,* the story of Babe Didrikson Zaharias—I had no idea, first of all, how my acting would be built around the whole idea that I could actually play golf. It took many takes for me to sink a 16-foot putt. We kept persevering, and finally it went in, and it was a shot from the movie that was used on a lot of posters.

I hit a ball with an iron about as far as I do with a wood—so I'm really no golfer. I was completely intimidated from attempting to learn the sport for years, because I was invited to participate in so many tournaments. I had never played a game of golf. I had learned how to swing the club and look like I knew what I was doing, and I had studied Babe enough so I that I could focus on what the facial and body expressions were. And I had a wonderful coach, Nicky Sholdar, and I'm amazed that 15 years later people are still talking about this movie. The film truly is some kind of a classic.

I've never picked up a club since. Bless him, the late George Zaharias persuaded Wilson to send me my own golf bag with my name on it, and clubs, which everybody has used—except for me, of course. All my stepsons have borrowed them. (They're hackers, but they have a good time.) To be perfectly honest, if I lived in an area that's not as polluted as Los Angeles, I would be out playing a lot more than I am. But golf is a game that you should play in wonderful, quality air. It doesn't matter if it's hot or cold, but especially if you play badly, the air should be clean because you're doing so much walking and breathing.

Susan Clark has starred in 20 feature films. "Babe" earned Susan an Emmy as Best Actress. She and co-star Alex Karras married, and formed a production company, Georgian Bay Productions.

Ben Crenshaw

DELICACY

My story concerns a high-spirited oilman from West Texas with more money than brains, and more desire than talent. Someone must have told him about the famed teacher Harvey Penick, so the next thing you know he jumps in a plane and flies to Austin in order to take a lesson on the short game from Mr. Penick. The practice green was nearby and

30

Mr. Penick began by having the excitable man hit a few light chips with a seven-iron.

Sure enough the man began to hit tops, shanks, and blades across the green onto the cart path. Mr. Penick interceded softly, as he always does, and said, "Mr. Smith, these little shots need to be a little more delicate. You need to try and use your little muscles. Let's try and pretend that you are a jeweler, and I would give you my finest gold watch, and that you would try and fix it, being as delicate as you can."

The man said, "Sure."

He then proceeded to top, chili-dip, and skull chip after chip. After a few more, Mr. Penick said, "Well, we better go on to something else," and the man asked, "What will I do now?" Mr. Penick said, "You can do something for me, can't you?" The man replied, "Certainly!" and Mr. Penick asked, "May I please have my watch back?"

Ben Crenshaw is one of the most loved golfers ever, by fans and peers alike. Harvey Penick has been his teacher since Ben was a little boy. Ben's amateur record shows three NCAA championship titles and the 1973 Western Amateur championship. As a professional, Ben has won 15 titles, including the 1984 Masters. He has represented the U.S. in three Ryder Cups.

Donna de Varona
THE BIGGEST SHOT OF MY LIFE

Capital Cities/ABC, Inc.

My one and only attempt to play golf occurred at the Dinah Shore Colgate-Palmolive Golf Tournament in Palm Springs, California. It was in the mid-1970s when David Foster, CEO of Colgate-Palmolive, helped push women's sports ahead "one giant leap" by sponsoring numerous women's sports events.

This tournament even included a fashion show in which the top golfers, like Carol Mann and Hollis Stacy, along with

notable athletes from other sports, modeled the latest in
women's sportswear. A fish out of water, my biggest concern
was not stumbling on the runway. At least that was my focus
up until the time Hollis and my brother invited me out on the
course.

My brother Kurt, by the way, is a teaching pro. He has
played golf since he was six and has an unbelievable swing
that helped him beat the great Tom Watson in a round of golf.
Kurt was 16 years old at the time.

I didn't exactly play the first two holes. I just swung as
hard as I could and missed. With every swing I got more and
more frustrated; the ball just didn't seem to be that small. My
self-esteem plummeted with each hole. The more I tried, the
worse I got. Hollis and Kurt, however, were unflappable and
kept giving me their best hints.

We then got to a hole with a water hazard. I must have
felt comfortable near my element, because when I teed off I
made easily the best swing of my life. I connected and hit that
ball clear over the water; it landed right next to the pin. Hollis
and Kurt went nuts and so did I. It was then that I clearly
understood the term "golf addiction." I walked up and suc-
cessfully tapped the ball in for a birdie. And that was it. I
decided it was just too easy and gave up the game.

Actually, years later I did go out to Kurt's golf range in
Los Gatos, California, hoping to capture that special feeling
once again. He started to help me with my swing but when
I looked around for some additional coaching and found him
flat out on the ground laughing hysterically, I knew I had

33

made the right decision, at least for now. But then again wouldn't it be nice to some day score just one more birdie.

Donna de Varona as a teenager won two gold medals in the 1964 Olympic Games. Her record-breaking career included 18 world records, which gained her entry into the Olympic, Women's Sports Foundation and Swimming Halls of Fame. The youngest and first woman full-time network sportscaster on television, she has used her visibility to help others. As a founder and president of the Women's Sports Foundation, and as a Special Consultant to the U.S. Senate, she has helped enact legislation that has improved the opportunities for both girls and boys in sports and physical fitness.

⚑ Joe Dey

JACK NICKLAUS' PUZZLEMENT

United States Golf Association

As a referee I have had the opportunity to watch close up as the finest golfers ply their trade. I got to know surprising things about them. For example, Jack Nicklaus keeps a super-serious face when he's in the midst of something big, but he keeps his sense of humor always. Such was the case during a late round of match play in the United States Amateur Championship of 1961 at the Pebble Beach Golf Links in California.

The eighth hole is a magnificent, unorthodox par-four. It swings above and around an arm of the Pacific called Carmel Bay. Players flirt with adventure if they aren't sure of their ground. Long hitters usually lay up their drives near the brink of the fairway as it rises from the tee. There are other avenues, such as playing well to the left, but there's not much inviting fairway.

So Nicklaus and his opponent both laid up close to the fairway's brow.

Dead ahead, between the fairway and putting green, rock headlands fall precipitously some 60 yards straight down to enclose a formidable water hazard. The narrow left fairway tempers down a bit, but whatever way the player chooses he faces a daunting shot. To go straight for the green may require most players to use four-, five- or six-irons onto a small, tightly bunkered green. It can be a bit hard to concentrate on your shot knowing sure death awaits the person who stumbles over the rocks.

It was my job to determine who was away, farther from the pin, therefore the next player to shoot. I couldn't tell by eyeballing it, so I proposed tossing a coin.

"No," chuckled the murderous Mr. Nicklaus. "Why don't you pace it off?"

The late **Joseph C. Dey, Jr.,** was the longtime executive director of the USGA. He became the PGA Tour's first Commissioner. He was one of the few Americans to hold the honor of being selected captain of the R & A at St. Andrews, Scotland. Later in life, Joe taught ethics to sixth-grade boys at a private school on Long Island, New York.

Phyllis Diller

GOLF AND PAIN

Marc Raboy

My son seriously considered going to med school. He even bought a set of golf clubs. Right away he got the feeling that the reason the pro tells you to keep your head down is so you can't see him laughing. He was a quick learner and after only three lessons he could throw his golf clubs as far as other people who'd been playing for years. He said, "Mother, golf has taught me that there is a connection between pain and pleasure. Golf spelled backwards is flog." And he says when you consider the expense of golf clubs, green fees and cart rentals, it's hard to believe this game was invented in Scotland.

Phyllis Diller is a world-famous comedienne and author.

Bob Drum
AN EARLY INTRODUCTION

Steve Wilson

I think I can pinpoint when and where my life did an about-face and sent me into the world of golf—a world, by the way, I cherish for all the great moments I have had.

The year was 1946 and the place was the Longue Vue club in suburban Pittsburgh, the site of the Western Pennsylvania Junior championship. I was on assignment for the *Pittsburgh Press,* an assignment that I really hated. What the hell was I doing at a golf tournament for juvenile delinquents when the Pirates were playing baseball?

In the era of the Depression, when I was roaming the streets of Brooklyn, it was every kid's ambition to be a major league player, including mine. We lived and died with the Trolley Dodgers, as the team was known; a kindly man named Wilbert Robinson was the manager. So well liked was he that one year they called the team the Robins.

Golf was something you did on weekends by carrying the bag for a bunch of rich guys. I did my share of caddying. For this enterprise we were paid a dollar, from which the caddy master took 15 cents. The tips ranged in amounts from zero to a dollar. Only one guy tipped a dollar and it was known as the "gold loop." Most were just a dime.

It was necessary to go out to Seawane Country Club both days in order to get enough money to take the girl next door out on Saturday to the movies (25 cents) with a Coke (5 cents), and on Sunday to the tea dance (50 cents a couple).

I hated caddying and so did most of my confreres. Instead of learning to hit the curve ball or shagging flies or grounders, you had to spend all day at the club waiting for a chance to watch silly old men, with no athletic ability, try to hit a small ball.

I mention all this to set the stage for the about-face that occurred that summer day at Longue Vue. I had a taste of covering the baseball beat, and, except for playing the game, in those days it was the next thing to going to heaven.

I used to skip most of these local tournaments and rewrite the morning paper story as it was no big deal. In those days the only people who read about golf were the players themselves. But this day, a friend of mine and a fine toper, Frank Rhodes, had a son playing in the tournament so we went together for a day of watching golf from the tap room.

It was in the tap room (where I have learned many things by accident) that I heard tales about a phenom from Latrobe, a suburban town, the multi-talented son of a pro greenskeeper. The aficionados of the game were vociferous in their praise of young Arnold Palmer and aroused my latent interest.

The next thing you know, a report came to the clubhouse that Palmer was losing to some kid named Billy Zigo. And the unknown eventually conquered our hero.

Rhodes and I continued our visit and when his son won, he took off to give fatherly advice for the next round. I decided to go write my story and go to the baseball game that night.

I never got to the baseball game. On my way out, I saw a kid with five buckets of balls on the practice range, hitting them with a vicious cut and with a grimace on his face that indicated that the golf ball was his mortal enemy.

It was the first time I saw Palmer in my life and it has fostered a friendship that has lasted 45 years to date and is still going. I decided to talk with Palmer and ask what happened.

"I just got beat," was his candid answer. "I didn't play well and I blame myself. I wasn't ready and thought this tournament was a breeze. I thought I could win without playing.

"Let me tell you this," Palmer continued. "I'm not going

to ever get beat again by being unprepared. This day has taught me a lesson."

It sure did. Never again would Arnold Palmer come not ready to play and each opponent and each golf course got his undivided attention. I think that is part of his charm. He never gives up.

It was years later when I saw Arnold on the steps of the clubhouse at Oakmont Country Club. He had spent four years in the Coast Guard and was pursuing an amateur career, not intending at the time to turn professional.

"I missed the cut here, Bob," he said. "Do you think I have a chance to beat these guys?" This was the Open Championship. Palmer was talking about Ben Hogan, Sam Snead, and a bunch of other Hall of Famers who were entered.

"Arnold, you can win any tournament you play in." I said it and I meant it.

While other people were telling him to stay as an amateur, I told him at the Country Club of Detroit while we were sitting alone after his winning the Amateur Championship that his only move was to turn professional.

"I have made up my mind to do just that," he answered. He was 25 years old at the time and his cash reserve was not very big. But, as we know, that changed abruptly.

So there you have it. Arnold Palmer didn't change my life. I owe it all to Frank Rhodes and his expense account and a kid named Billy Zigo. If he hadn't beat Palmer that day, I never would have been lucky enough to make a career out of going to golf tournaments.

Bob Drum has been Arnold Palmer's Boswell for nearly 50 years. And he has contributed to the fun and personality of golf through newspapers, magazines, and CBS television's "Drummer's Beat."

Betty Ford

THE GOLF WIDOW

Russell W. Ohlsen

I knew that Jerry loved golf from the time we first dated. But I was not a golfer and had no intention of becoming a golfer. My main interest had been in modern dance and fashion work. I did take up skiing in order for us to spend time together and that enhanced our relationship, because Jerry loved to ski. We lived in Michigan at that time and on winter weekends he wanted to go north and hit the slopes. As a fashion coordinator, I had a fashion show every Saturday at noon. I really had to hustle to get out to go skiing with him.

At the beginning of our marriage, golf was something Jerry didn't have a lot of time for. He was new in his career as a Member of Congress from Michigan, so he couldn't get around to playing much golf, except on an occasional Sunday. Then he would play with a few other Congressmen—the members called their group "Chowder and Marching."

When the four Ford children came of school age, I finally took my first golf lessons. This gave me the opportunity to play one morning a week with my contemporaries. I really enjoyed being out on the course. It can be a pretty therapeutic place when you have four very active children at home!

Occasionally, Jerry and I would spend a weekend at the Greenbriar to play golf together. I was always frightened on that first tee. All those wonderful golfers lined up waiting to tee off. I wanted to be able to play well enough to keep up with my husband, but of course I couldn't. Jerry has a powerful long shot, particularly off the tee. He was very patient while waiting for me to take my three strokes to catch up with him, but I could sense his feeling of frustration. I don't think husbands are very good teachers for wives. We need to go to our own pro and take our own lessons . . . and that goes for most sports.

Some of Jerry's favorites on the golf course are the greats, like Bob Hope, Jack Nicklaus and Arnie Palmer. They are good friends, too. He also plays quite a bit with Leonard Firestone and Dee Keaton. He likes the game and the camaraderie of the game—the fun of getting together and being out there with the guys.

43

He also likes the challenge of going out and trying to win. We all like to win. When he leaves, I usually say to him, "It's not how hard you hit it, honey. It's how easy." He sort of shudders and says, "Thanks. Yes, I know." Jerry Ford has a fairly competitive spirit. Even though he plays golf for the pleasure of it, he'll get more pleasure if he wins. And besides, he always shares his winnings with me . . . and I never have to help cover his losses.

When we moved to California, it was "supposedly" because there were so many golf courses in the Rancho Mirage area. The idea was that Jerry would play more since he was retired. Well, he's never quite gotten the hang of "retirement." He still spends a good deal of time traveling, giving lectures and attending meetings. But at least when he is home, if he has the time, the courses are right outside the door.

Jerry plays in quite a few tournaments sponsored by friends and for good causes. There's the Bob Hope Desert Classic, Tip O'Neill's tournament up in Cape Cod, the Danny Thomas tournament for St. Jude's Hospital, the Los Angeles Children's Hospital tournament and a gathering each summer in Vail, Colorado for something called the Jerry Ford Invitational.

A few years ago, the question came up about me becoming involved in a tournament to raise funds for the Betty Ford Center. While it was a wonderful opportunity to raise money for my favorite cause, I didn't want to impinge on his territory. We finally decided that since I wasn't going to be playing—my bad back and neck forced me to give up golf years ago—the Betty Ford Invitational Golf Tournament was a good idea. The Betty Ford is played on the Monday following the Nabisco Dinah Shore. Like the Dinah, it features players from the Ladies Professional Golf Association. This year marks our sixth annual tournament.

Jerry is really a very good golfer, but his reputation, helped along by the monologues of his good friend and golf partner Bob Hope, might lead you to believe otherwise. Bob long ago suggested that Jerry doesn't know which golf course he's going to play until he tees off. He once joked, "Jerry Ford told me he was playing better. Just yesterday he got a birdie, an eagle, an elk, a moose and a Mason."

Jerry has been able to incorporate Bob's quips into his own speeches, and he always gets a laugh. He got in a good barb when he complained, "Bob, you're going to have to get some new material. People are getting tired of me telling these same old golf stories."

Dolores Hope and I have often talked about our husbands traveling so much. We've kidded about getting together to write a book about Bob and Jerry. We'd call it *Guess Who I Saw at the Airport?* That's where the two of them seem to spend most of their time.

There may have been times when I resented Jerry playing golf, because it left me alone. But I really love to have him play. It's such a healthy thing. And even if he doesn't always come home in the best mood, it's worth it.

Betty Ford has appeared on the list of Most Admired Women for the past 16 years. She is a leader in drug prevention and rehabilitation.

President Gerald R. Ford

FAVORITE FOURSOMES

Whenever Bob Hope and I are together, you can be assured that he will always have something illuminating to say about my golf game. He is the only comedian I know who has a black belt in compliments. For example, several months ago we were playing golf and there was a huge crowd gathered to watch him tee off. A spectator yelled out to him, "Hey Bob, What's your favorite foursome?" Bob responded, "Jerry Ford, a faith healer, and a paramedic."

Anyway, every year in January, Bob Hope, Tip O'Neill and I play in a foursome in the Bob Hope Desert Classic. It's a four-day event and each day a different professional plays in the foursome.

There are 52 teams in the event. Several years ago, the team of Hope, O'Neill, and Ford finished 52nd. Obviously, our greatest talents are not on the golf course.

President Gerald R. Ford was the 38th President of the United States. He has played in more professional-amateur golf events than any other President. Each year President Ford hosts the Jerry Ford pro-am in Vail, Colorado, to raise money for charity and to have some laughs with his golfing friends.

Arthur Frommer

THE GOLF COURSES OF NORTHERN IRELAND

My most memorable association with golf was a visit I made several years ago to the two great golf courses of Northern Ireland: The Royal County Down and the Royal Portrush. These are two of the most challenging courses in all of the world. The first is on a wild, windswept cliff overlooking the sea, and the other is on equally rough inland terrain with all sorts of shrubs and grass growing wildly, swept as they are by gale-force winds. Once you have played here, going anywhere else is like returning to kindergarten.

What was so touching about the visit was the welcome I received from the club members who live a terribly isolated life because of the unrest in Belfast and Londonderry. The endless conflict in Northern Ireland has virtually ended normal tourism to Northern Ireland and yet once you leave the two major cities, you wouldn't know that anything is wrong. Everything is peaceful and the people are eager to greet you and make you feel welcome; they are especially desperate for the return of tourism and the resumption of the use of such facilities as Royal County Down and Royal Portrush by foreigners.

Both clubhouses have become a little behind the times, a little careworn. And yet, the greeting you receive is so strong and enthusiastic that it makes for a wonderful visit. They will turn themselves upside down to make things available for you, to provide you with a partner for going out on the links. I can think of no more remarkable an opportunity to play golf than in the two links of the major courses of Northern Ireland that are now so underutilized.

It is not difficult to get there. You can fly from any number of airports in the British Isles into Belfast and rent a car. And in no time at all, you can be playing on either of the two most challenging and memorable golf courses in all the world.

Arthur Frommer, the "Dean of American travel," has written *Europe on $40 a Day* (once *Europe on $5 a Day*) for the past 35 years. He publishes 128 titles dealing with every major travel destination in the world.

James Garner & Jack Garner

AS TOLD BY JACK GARNER

PLAYING A HOLE WITH YOUR NAME ON IT

Warner Brothers

This story comes from a golf tournament known as the Cherokee Strip Classic and it was played in Ponca City, Oklahoma during the mid-1960s. At that time, I was a golf pro at the Twin Lakes Golf Club in Norman, Oklahoma and Jim had come out from California to play in the pro-am with me. Our caddy at that time was a young kid named Doug. He couldn't

50

have been more than 10 or 12 years old—the bag was bigger than he was.

They'd had a shotgun start that day and our last hole would have been the second hole, which was a par three. All of the holes on the golf course were named after celebrities and on the tee markers were the names of the celebrities playing. When we reached the seventeenth hole, also a par three, we read the tee marker. It was the "James Garner" hole. At that point neither Jim or I had been playing well; in fact, we were way back in the pack. But somehow, seeing the tee marker sign with Jim's name in big letters brought us a wonderful spate of luck. I hit first, and made a nifty little hole-in-one. We picked up two shots. We moved on to the eighteenth hole, a par five, and Jim got a stroke on that hole. He hit two drivers, knocked it on the green, and made the putt for a net two. We then had picked up five shots in two holes.

We next headed off to the first hole, a par four, which I birdied. That gave us six shots. We then went to the last hole, which was a par three. I missed the green, Jim hit the left hand front corner of the green, and the pin was in the right back. It had to be a seventy footer if it was an inch. Jim made it. That gave us seven shots on the last four holes, and we finished in third place.

Prize money wasn't real big in those days, but they gave me $500 for my hole-in-one. Afterwards, back in the locker room, the redoubtable Jimmy Demaret asked me, "Jack, what club did you hit with on that hole-in-one?" It was a hole of approximately 150 yards, and I jokingly told him, "Oh, I just knocked it down with a little three-iron."

Demaret laughingly replied, "For God sakes, they should have given you the whole golf course if you hit a three-iron." Of course, I used a seven-iron, but who didn't love kidding Jimmy?

Probably the most remarkable thing about this story is not the hole-in-one or that we picked up so many shots, but who our caddy was. Doug's last name was Tewell and he has gone on to become a top pro. But we'll never let him forget we knew him when.

James Garner has starred in numerous movies, television series, and on the stage, doing everything from light comedy to serious drama.

Jack Garner has been a touring pro for years. He makes his home in Oklahoma.

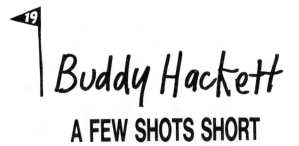

Buddy Hackett

A FEW SHOTS SHORT

Since Carol Mann asked me to tell a favorite golf story, I remember a time I was playing in a celebrity pro-am tournament at the Desert Inn in Las Vegas, back in the 1960s. I had an interesting night before, which started with me and a few pals drinking whiskey until three or four in the morning. At that point I decided I was hungry, so I got together with Louis Nye, who was working over at the Tropicana, and we went downtown for chili at Benny Binyon's Horseshoe Club.

Benny told us he'd had a guy who had lost $150,000 in his casino that night. And the guy told Benny, "You know why I'm such a lucky guy?" Knowing that this man had just lost a bundle, Benny said, "Why?" And the guy answered, "Cause your chili's 10 cents a bowl, and I love chili." (You know, Ben used to charge 10 cents a bowl just to get people into his place.)

Anyway, after we finished eating the chili, we were pretty bloated. I was driving Louis back, the sun was coming up, and all of a sudden I saw smoke rising up out of desert. And I said, "Louis, a plane crashed!" Good Samaritans that we were, we raced out into the desert. We raced and raced. And raced. We must have driven forty miles. Back in those days the desert air was so clean you couldn't tell how far away something was. Finally we came to a burning garbage dump. Imagine our disappointment at not finding a plane.

So we turned around, drove forty miles back to Vegas. I took Louis back to the Tropicana, and I said, "Well, now it's time for the tournament." So I went and showered, took a shave, put on some golf clothes and went over to the Desert Inn. I tried a few putts, met up with Carol, and went off to play. You could say I was a little the worse for wear. Hell, you could say I was still smashed out of my skin.

Anyway, I played so well I was reminded of the story of the guy who went up to Jimmy Demaret and said, "Jimmy, do you think I'm overgolfed?" And Jimmy said, "Take a few swings." So the guy did. And Jimmy advised, "You should lay off for nine days—and then give up the game entirely."

So there I was playing with Carol Mann, and she was wonderful. I remember telling her all day on the course that she was so wonderful I just wanted to give her a hug. "Carol, can I give you a hug?" "Sure," she said. So I got on my knees and grabbed her long, bare legs and hugged 'em. I didn't want to let go. You know, it sure was hard for her to play the next three holes that way.

I almost brought her down to my level.

While in my forties, all of a sudden I couldn't hit the long ball—and they started calling me "Long-not." I'm only 5′6″ but I used to be able to blast the ball about 240 yards. And then, all of a sudden, 211, 212—that's all I could get out of the drive. So I flew to see Jimmy Demaret in Houston, at the Champions, and I cried out, "Jiiiiiimmmmy! Jimmy, I can't hit the ball as far as I used to." Then he put his arm around me and said, "Well, Buuuuud, don't none of us hit the ball as far as we used to."

I was feeling better at the end. In fact, I parred 15, 16, 17, and 18. When asked why I couldn't do that well on the first fourteen holes, I answered, "The first fourteen didn't have cameras."

Buddy Hackett has starred in movies, on television (especially on cable and as a favorite of late night talk shows) and in nightclubs from Las Vegas to the Catskills.

Charlton Heston
CADDY NUMBER 256

I've never played golf, though I know it's a great game, enjoyed by millions all over the world, perhaps partly because it requires neither great athletic ability nor athletic condition, even at a world-class level. Jack Nicklaus, maybe the greatest player in the history of the game, was some 20 pounds overweight when he was dominating the world tour as "the Golden Bear."

I do play chess, though not very well. It seems to me Jack Nicklaus has more in common with Garry Kasparov than with Joe Montana. Though Nicklaus or Norman or Wadkins have to physically walk the course, club golfers are now largely required to ride in carts, half their shots tapped with a putter. My golfing friends tell me theirs is largely a mental game, like chess. I understand the pressures and the challenge this involves.

I did caddy for one summer when I was 13, at the Indian Hills Golf Club in a suburb of Chicago. My caddy number was 256. I was paid $1.50 a round. I guess I wasn't very good; the caddy-master almost never gave me more than one round a day. About my finest memory is that were apple trees on the thirteenth fairway. I often had time to put a couple of Winesaps in my pocket.

The next summer I worked in a steel mill. The work was a lot harder (a *lot* harder), but I was paid better, too. On balance, I preferred it to golf.

Charlton Heston has starred in over 50 feature films. His roles have included cardinals and cowboys, kings and quarterbacks, presidents and painters, cops and conmen, astronauts and geniuses—and have covered 5000 years of past and future history. Charlton served six terms as President of the Screen Actors Guild, after which he became chairman of the American Film Institute.

Bob Hope

SHOWMANSHIP

I've played golf with Nancy Lopez. I love to play with all the girls because we all use the same tee. The first time I played with Nancy, the first hole was about 390 yards and Nancy and I were in the same position hitting into the green, except it was her second shot and my fourth.

It's amazing how good the girls are and even more amazing how they can embarrass you when you stand up at the tee and that pretty thing that weighs 108 pounds can outdrive you by 25 yards.

You've got to use a lot of showmanship to live that down.

Bob Hope has logged almost as many hours on a golf course as he has performing and getting us to laugh. His stage, film, and television careers span nearly 80 years and have made him a legend, along with his contributions to the morale of U.S. troops scattered throughout the world during four wars and the peace in between.

Dolores Hope
BOB AND I

I started playing golf when I was eighteen. An aunt of mine, who was a very good golfer, started me playing and I wouldn't be surprised if golf is one of the reasons Bob wanted me for his wife. On the first date that we had, we spent most of the time talking, among other things, about courses we'd both played. And at the restaurant, we used a pencil to write on the tablecloth recollecting great golf holes, and not-so-great golf holes. I really think golf, and Scottie dogs, is what probably brought us together. We both had Scottie dogs.

My lowest handicap was a 6—but I only beat Bob once in our long marriage. Years and years ago, I went with Bob to Vienna to do the music recording of a movie. The golf course there was inside a horse track. When we went down to play, I played the best golf I've ever played in my life. We started to gather a crowd because the people there recognized Bob. By the time we got to the 18th, one of the big mouths who was following us stood up and said, "Here are the scores. We would like you all to know the score is Mr. Hope, 78; Mrs. Hope, 76." I knew I had a good marriage when Bob got a bigger kick out of that than I did.

My favorite golf story, though, occurred back in the 1940s, when Bobby Dawson was the California state champion. Her mother was the type of lady who didn't know a blessed thing about golf. Her family belonged to the country club at Piedmont for the sole purpose of lunching with the ladies while dressed in hats and lavender and old lace. Well, Bobby was playing in the state meet at Pebble Beach. The weather was bad that day, and at the eleventh hole, Bobby found herself with an unplayable lie that cost her the match.

While lunching at the club the next day, Bobby's mother was asked by the other ladies, "How did Bobby do?" She responded, "She was doing fine until she got to the eleventh fairway when she had an unavoidable lay."

Dolores Hope has given her support to various charities, including the exquisite Eisenhower Medical Center in Rancho Mirage, CA. She is a terrific cook, especially of Italian food. Dolores' infectious sense of humor makes her easy to be around. Her golf has been enthusiastic enough so that the tournament players made her an honorary member of the LPGA.

Hale Irwin

A ROCKY SHOT

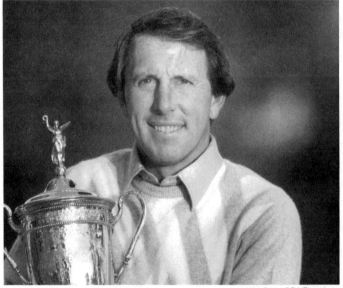

Jeff McBride, PGA Tour photo

In 1984, at the last Crosby Invitational (before AT&T became the title sponsor), I won, but I won in such a *different* way. I hadn't been playing particularly well throughout the week, in terms of hitting quality golf shots time after time. I'd either hit a great golf shot or a terrible golf shot. I could never seem to get myself on an even keel in terms of shot production. However, I managed as many birdies as bogies, so I managed to hang in there.

On the last day, I'd played my typical up-and-down game, but I was in the lead. When it came down to the last few holes where it would be decided as to who would win and who would lose, it looked as if I was going to lose. Jim Nelford had taken the lead. When I came to the last hole I needed to make a birdie.

At the tee, I decided to hit a high-risk shot down the left side near the ocean so I could get my second shot in a better position to hit my third. Those shots were all connected. I failed miserably with the tee shot and pull-hooked it. As I was standing there, forlornly looking to see where it last crossed the hazard so I'd know where to drop it, the ball came bounding back towards the fairway. Amazingly it hit a rock, and bounced exactly the right way. That was break number one.

Then I hit probably the best three-wood of my career in terms of distance and placement to get it down the fairway where I had a sand wedge to the green. My caddy said, "Why don't we just hole it? Then we don't have to worry about a play-off."

I couldn't quite oblige him, but that third shot did hit the pin, and drop down about five feet from the hole. I had one of those TV tap-ins for my tying birdie.

We went on to the first play-off hole at the fifteenth. Jim and I both played it extremely well. The putt I had for what was then a win on the first hole was about twenty feet behind the hole. I'd missed that putt, exactly the same putt, an hour earlier. I'd missed it on the low side, so the second time around I knew how to break it. I planned to hit it up a little higher, and hit it exactly where I wanted it. It stayed up on the high side.

Then I proceeded to the sixteenth tee shot, where I skied a three-wood—a very poor shot. In fact, the television crews thought I was in the far right-hand bunker where indeed I would have been dead. I wasn't fortunate enough, however, to have hit it even that far. In fact, I could probably have hit a six-iron as far as I hit that three-wood. From that point, I was some 194 yards away from the pin. I was in a bunker, had a pretty good lie, and had to go a little bit left to right. My first thought was to go for it. My second thought was to lay it up. It was back into the wind and I didn't think a three-iron would get that far. Going with my first impression, I went with a two-iron and got the ball within 10 feet of the cup. It ended up being a great golf shot—the epitome of how I had been playing that week: a very poor shot followed by a very great shot.

My win and less-than-standard play got more than the usual attention. The story ran in the *Sports Illustrated* swimsuit issue—so years later people still remember my shot off the rock.

Hale Irwin has won three U.S. Opens, two Memorials, and 14 other events on some of America's toughest courses. He has appeared on five Ryder Cup teams. Besides a gifted intellect, Hale has a silly side that can tickle you no end. Hale has recently expanded his business interests to include golf course design.

Peter Jacobsen

STREAKING THE BRITISH OPEN

Tom Treick

The rich, 130-year tradition of the British Open has seen some of the greatest moments in golf history: the six victories of Harry Vardon in the early 1900s . . . Ben Hogan's last major championship in 1953 . . . the incomparable Arnold Palmer's back-to-back wins in 1961–62 . . . my bone-crushing tackle on the final hole in 1985 . . . Greg Nor—

What?

You've never heard of my tackle? Oh, it was something. Dick Butkus would have been proud.

First, a little background on the British Open. This tournament is the greatest event in golf. The experience of playing the links courses in England and Scotland—built centuries ago with such simple equipment—can be overwhelming. These courses have weathered over time, and this unique design aspect forces you to play many types of imaginative shots.

Here in the United States, we have beautifully manicured golf courses, irrigated fairways and greens where the ball will stop on a dime. We play "target golf"—that is, we hit the ball in the air and try to land on the spot we want to stop, much like throwing darts.

You can't do this in Great Britain. If you do, the links courses will eat you alive. You *must* survey the course and play the bounces of the fairways and greens. A perfectly struck shot can bounce off a hump; the difference between birdie and bogey can depend on which side of the hump you hit.

The weather also adds to the excitement and atmosphere of the British Open. I must say, when the weather is nice, I'm a little disappointed. I want the weather to be nasty and windy like it is in the history books. When the wind is up, it really makes for creative play. I enjoy the challenge.

Royal St. George, the site of the 1985 Open, epitomizes the links courses. The deep swells and mounds and tricky spots around the greens—and the usual strong winds—can take a player completely out of his game plan. But if you know your way around, you can play the shots that will bounce to your benefit. This means that everybody has the ability to play well—long hitters and short hitters alike.

I was playing very well that year at Royal St. George. On the final day, I was near the lead, in the last four or five groups. As usual, the wind was blowing. My playing partner, Tom Kite, shot a 33 on the front nine for a two-stroke lead. As we began the back nine, however, Tom had a double bogey, and I simply ran out of gas. As we teed off on the eighteenth hole, we were still in contention, though just barely. Sandy Lyle, playing in the group behind us, had a two- or three-stroke lead.

The eighteenth hole at Royal St. George is a long par four, about 440 yards, and it was directly into the wind. Tom and I both missed the green with our second shots. As we walked up to survey our pitch shots, suddenly a guy came sprinting out of the crowd behind the green.

He was buck naked.

I couldn't believe it. A streaker at the British Open. Sacrilege!

He ran on the fringe on the back of the green toward Tom Kite, made a circle, ran past Tom, past me, and back to where he had started. There were no officials anywhere.

At first, the crowd sat in stunned silence. After a few seconds, though, they broke into an uproarious ovation of laughing and cheering. Tom was laughing. I was laughing. We looked at the crowd, threw our arms up in the air, and enjoyed the hilarity of the moment.

Our hero was having so much fun, he decided to take a second lap around the green. Tom and I and our caddies, Mike Cowan and Mike Carrick, congregated on the front of the green. I put my arm around Tom, though as we stood there chuckling, we couldn't forget the business at hand. We both had tough pitch shots to contend with, and didn't want to drop any further off the lead.

We weren't ever going to get to hit those shots, however, as long as our streaker friend kept hogging the spotlight. As he came around for his third lap, we were all wondering how long this was going to go on. Finally, the bobbies, in their big, heavy boots, came out to chase him around. It looked like a scene out of "Abbott and Costello Meet the Keystone Cops."

This was getting ridiculous. They weren't anywhere near catching the guy, and I was becoming concerned about the surface of the green and all the ugly boot marks that were appearing. Something had to be done. Action had to be taken!

The streaker dodged and weaved and worked his way past Kite and over to where Mike Cowan and I were standing. I leaned over to Mike and told him my plan. Mike just laughed and said, "Yeah, right."

As he ran toward me, I dropped down into my best Lawrence Taylor impersonation. Fourth and goal. The streaker gave me a couple of head fakes, but an experienced linebacker doesn't fall for those. As he tried to run to my right, I flew toward him and hit him around the knees (given his choice of apparel, I didn't want to hit him any higher than that). He flew into the air, hit the ground with a thud, and the bobbies piled on.

The crowd went nuts (they've been hooked on American football ever since), but I didn't notice. I was too busy looking for the fumble. Finding no loose football, I did my best Mark

Gastineau sack dance and strutted around the green.

To this day, I still can't believe I did that. Why did I do it? Well, the guy was walking on my line.

I eventually chipped up and missed my par putt. However, I feel confident that no one has ever has received such an ovation after a bogey.

If I win a major championship someday, I'll never achieve the instant notoriety that I received following my goal-line stand.

I had a pretty good year in 1985. Not only did I finish 23rd on the money list, but I led the Tour in tackles.

Peter Jacobsen may have provided more laughs on the PGA Tour than Lee Trevino. A very creative man, Peter is renowned for his hilarious impersonations of his fellow Tour players. Though he may be most proud of his singular football accomplishment, he's also a pretty good golfer. Peter has won five tournaments, including the 1990 Bob Hope Chrysler Classic.

Charlie Jones

GOOD OLD WHAT'S-HIS-NAME

In 1966, the second year that I was with NBC Sports, I drew one of the premier assignments, the Bob Hope Chrysler Classic in the Palm Springs area. The reason this was such a choice assignment is that at that time Chrysler Corporation was the sole sponsor of the Bob Hope Classic, and also the sponsor of half of all sports on NBC. So it was really a heavyweight event for us, and of course it still is.

I was living in Dallas, and when I got the news I called my friend, the great golfer Mickey Wright, to have lunch and discuss the Bob Hope Classic. She filled me in on the players, the background of the tournament, and the golf courses. I then read everything I could find, the complete PGA guide, and all the golf magazines I could get my hands on so that when I got to Palm Springs I would be ready. I had information coming out of my suitcases.

On Saturday we were broadcasting from La Quinta. We were on for one hour, and I was stationed at the bottom of the tower at the eighteenth hole. I was to read the opening billboards ("The Bob Hope Classic is brought to you by Chrysler," etc., etc., etc.). Then I was to do an update at the 30-minute mark, some interviews near the end of the hour telecast, and take us off the air.

At the top of the telecast, I read the opening billboards, which lasted 20 seconds, and that was the last thing that I did. I waited and waited and waited, but they never came back to me. I was absolutely crushed. I went back to my room at the Erawan Garden Hotel, which is still there on Highway 111, and just went into hiding. I didn't even feel like venturing out of my room. The phone rang, and it was Mickey Wright. She said, "Charlie, you were absolutely fantastic." I said, "Mickey, how can you say that? I only did 20 seconds." She said, "But you did them so well." Then she added, "I learned a long time ago only to worry about the things I can control. When I'm playing in a golf tournament, I can only worry about my golf game and not what the other golfer might be doing. So you need only concern yourself with what you did when they came to you. That may have been only for 20 seconds, but you were absolutely magnificent." Of course, this really buoyed my spirits, so I went back to work, gathering all the material for Sunday, the final round.

That Sunday, I was at the fifteenth hole, a par three, at Indian Wells, and I had enough notes taped on the scaffolding, the monitor, and to the table in front of me that I could have done three hours on the fifteenth hole alone. I remember it's the famous par three they call the $50,000 hole, where Don January had a hole-in-one that had been insured by Lloyds of London. They call it "The Golf Shot Heard Around the World." I had all kinds of information like that.

As we came on the air, I was sitting on the tower at 15, and again I'm to read the opening billboards. As I said "The Bob Hope Desert Classic is brought to you by Chrysler," etc., etc., etc., the last threesome of the day was putting out on 15. So when I got through with the opening billboards, that was it. There were no more golfers. They were all on 16, 17 and 18. Needless to say, I was crushed again. How could this possibly happen two days in a row?

Then, with the best turn of events that an announcer can ever have in a golf tournament, Arnold Palmer and Doug Sanders tied, and they went into sudden death.

The first sudden death started at the fifteenth tee.

My hole.

I'm ready.

During the delay while Arnie and Doug signed their scorecards and then were driven out to the 15th, our director punched up a shot of Dwight David Eisenhower, who was present in the gallery at 18. This was the first time the Eisenhower Trophy was being awarded, and the General was there to make the presentation. Our producer, Lou Kusserow, shouted in my ear, "Monitor, monitor." So naturally I looked to the monitor and he said, "There's the late president."

Well, I knew that the word "late" was incorrect, but I could not think of the word "former." And in the process, I forgot the man's name. So I said, "There he is." There was this long silence in my ear, followed by several expletives from Lou.

Luckily, the players were now on the tee at 15, and I waxed eloquent about the hole. Doug Sanders hit his tee shot on the green and Arnold missed the green and was down the right side, below the trap.

As the golfers started walking up the fairway, Lou Kusserow decided he'd try it again and shouted in my ear, "Monitor, monitor." I looked to the monitor, and he said in a very strident voice, "The *late* president." Again I knew that "late" was incorrect, but I still could not think of the word "former," and in the process, I still could not remember the name of the most famous man in the world, so I said, "There he is, again."

Just as a footnote, Doug Sanders parred the hole, Arnie bogied it, Sanders won, and I was off to a shaky start in my golf broadcasting career at NBC.

Charlie Jones is one of the most versatile, well-prepared voices of the modern sports era. A very pleasant man, Charlie now hosts NBC's golf coverage, along with NFL football, and swimming and diving at the 1992 Barcelona Olympics.

James S. Kemper, Jr.

DREAM ON, GOLFER, DREAM ON!

Kemper Group first sponsored the Kemper Open on the PGA Tour in June 1968. As president of the company, I felt this was a good advertising vehicle for us and a good way to increase "brand name" recognition at a reasonable cost. One little anomaly—the company president didn't play golf. I hadn't played in many years, and really had little interest in playing.

The following April, my wife and I were vacationing at Mauna Kea, Hawaii. April 8 was my fifty-fifth birthday. I said, "You know, we sponsor a PGA tournament, and I should really show some personal interest in golf. I think I'm old enough to start playing golf again. I'll give it a try." So I rented clubs and shoes and went out to the course with Al Cole, a friend of mine who was then Chairman of Reader's Digest and a pretty good golfer.

I think I shot 137, or maybe it was 147, I'm not sure. But on the ninth hole, (oh, happy day!) a miracle happened. This is a par four, about 380 yards from the white tees. You drive over a canyon and the second shot is slightly downhill to a well-trapped green. I hit the only decent drive I had all day and then knocked a four-wood into the hole. An eagle 2!

I went back up to the room and said to my wife, "Golf is really a simple game, nothing to it and I think I'll start playing again." I did. I still am and I love it. I don't play very well, but I have become a total addict. I can't tell you how much Kemper has since spent sponsoring the men's and women's events—because I don't know exactly. Still, that has had to be the most expensive eagle ever made.

Of course, that was my first and, up to now, my last eagle on a par four hole. But golfers are dreamers. I'm only 77, so I have plenty of time. Just maybe, some day, somewhere, on an island in the Pacific or on a course just around the corner from my home, lightning will strike again and I'll see my second shot disappear into the hole for another eagle two.

James S. Kemper, Jr., has been one of those quiet yet effective corporate leaders for decades in America. His sincere and disciplined approach to any task has made many charities the beneficiary of his efforts. Since retiring from Kemper Group, Jim maintains close involvement in sports through Kemper Sports, Inc.

Joanna Kerns

CHIP-OFF TO EUROPE

I started playing golf when I was in my late twenties. My ex-husband bought me a set of clubs and a series of lessons. He loved golf. Playing golf was the only place we didn't fight. We had great trips and vacations together. One of the things we fought over in the divorce was our club membership—and I lost. Women have very few rights in this sport. It's so frustrating. I've been divorced about six years. So now I just accept invitations to play and I hint a lot. My handicap fluctuates around 18.

As a single woman living in golf-starved southern California, I have not been able to find a club that will allow me to join. I don't really have much of a chance to improve except for invitations to play in celebrity tournaments. At a recent Steve Garvey Make-A-Wish Foundation Invitational in Hawaii, some, but not all, of my golf dreams came true.

Since I hadn't played in a few months, I took a crash lesson from Bob Harrison at Brentwood before going to Hawaii. He did a little thing to my swing and I played fantastically. For me to play in the high 80s or low 90s is spectacular. I was doing everything right and managed to sail through the tournament, helping my team a lot each day.

Finally we got to the very last round where the format was an alternate-shot, two-person team shootout. One team would be eliminated at the end of each hole. Steve Garvey was my partner. He was playing pretty well but because I wasn't really a terrific competitor I figured we'd be out of the contest during the early holes. I had no pressure on me. But my "new" game kept working for me. I was competing and holding my own with all of these seasoned athletes like Gary Morris, Matthew Lawrence, Jan Stenerud. The level of competition was overwhelming. My adrenalin flow was way up there. I was having a great time while those big guys were dropping like flies. On every hole somebody important self-destructed.

Going into the last hole it was Steve and me against Jan Stenerud and his partner. One of the tournament organizers mentioned, "Joanna, you're playing for a roundtrip ticket for two to Europe and it's between you and Jan.'' My thoughts got a little crazy, like "Who cares about Europe! I want to beat these monsters!''

We tied the last hole. In order to break the tie, Jan and I did the customary "chip-off'' from a little knoll over a sand trap, about a 20-yard shot. I wasn't really nervous. It was the first time I thought about winning because all along I was just having a good time. It was a shot I wasn't used to doing very often though. I played first, and in mid-swing looked up for the moon. The ball dribbled off the toe of the club and rolled into the sand trap. I was mortified. Jan seemed to spend a lifetime focusing on that ball. He played a great shot and that was that.

Later I came to realize how screwed up my priorities were. I wasn't angry that Jan Stenerud played better golf than me. I was angry because I felt sure I would have enjoyed Europe more than he did.

Joanna Kerns is the star of "Growing Pains," a situation comedy on ABC-TV. She is also the sister of Donna de Varona, Olympic gold medal swimmer. Joanna was a nationally-ranked gymnast when she was younger.

Jack Lemmon

MY GREATEST MOMENTS

    I first took up golf around 1960 and committed a cardinal sin. I didn't take any lessons. As a result, I managed to groove a swing that was filled with no-no's and I didn't even know it. At any rate, Bing heard that I had taken up the game and in 1963 he was kind enough to invite me to play in my first Crosby tournament. I had played in exactly one pro-am tourney prior to that in which I was partnered with Gay Brewer and I was so nervous that I missed my tee-off time because I drove to the wrong course. So you can imagine the state I was in as I approached the opening day of the most famous pro-am tournament in the world. I can't even remember who my pro partner was, but he was a rabbit on the tour—meaning it was damn near his first tournament, too. I practiced Monday till the sun went down. I practiced Tuesday till the sun went down. I practiced Wednesday till the sun went down. On Thursday there was no sun—it poured. It's all sort of a wet blur to me at this point, but I do know we started at Cypress Point, and I was approximately 15 over par through the first five holes. (As far as I was concerned, I was holding my own.)

By now the course resembled one huge swamp and although there had been several delays, play had not been suspended. After one of the delays we were finally able to tee off on the par-five sixth. I hit my drive slightly fat—meaning it went a snappy 130 to 140 yards. I laced into my next one and squirted it up to the top of the hill. At this point I was better than one-third of the way to the green and things were looking terrific. I hit a three-wood as hard as I could and actually picked it fairly clean but it sliced right and ended up about 120 yards from the green, in an absolute quagmire by the edge of the woods. I could see a tiny white speck of white in the mud which I identified as my ball and said to myself, "Take an eight-iron, hit behind the ball like you were in a sand trap, follow all the way through and let that little sucker float down onto the green." I did just that but the ball and the mud stuck to the club, and when I stopped my swing it "floated" all right, but it went backwards about 30 or 40 yards. Frankly, I don't think anyone has ever been able to duplicate that shot.

Back I trudged and I don't remember what club I used but I hit my best shot of the day, and when the ball sailed over the green it was still on the rise. Despite the rotten weather, there were still a few hardy souls that constituted a gallery. They were squatting on the side of the hill behind the green. As my pistol shot approached, bodies and umbrellas cascaded down that hill like they had been shot out of a cannon. My ball is still missing, and I think some of the people are, too.

The next hole was a short par three with an extremely deep and awesome trap on the right. Naturally I went in it. When we got to the trap, the ball was sitting in what looked like a small pond. I was allowed to place it out of the water— but of course still in the trap. I took my sand wedge, marched into the trap, began wiggling both feet to get them firmly planted, and kept wiggling while I mulled over the shot. After about 30 seconds of mulling I realized that I was in quicksand up to my ankles and I had better hit the damn thing before the shaft of the club was up to my Adam's apple. I hit a beautiful shot. It cleared the lip of the trap, cleared the green, cleared the gallery, and it's still somewhere in the woods. By now my feet were at least six inches in the wet sand and I couldn't lift either of them out. My caddy leaned over the edge of the trap and said, "Hand me your club and hold onto the end of it." He pulled, I held on, and out I came—minus one shoe. As far as I know, no one has ever recovered that shoe and I played the next couple of holes in one shoe and

81

a sock until a kind soul brought me another pair of shoes from the clubhouse.

Things did not improve during the ensuing holes and when we played Spyglass Hill the next day, at the end of the round my pro said, "That's a shame. You didn't play as well as you did yesterday."

If I told you everything that happened to me playing Pebble Beach the next day you'd swear it was fiction, so let's just cut to the fourteenth. That's where the cameras first picked me up. For those remaining five holes I got more coverage than Joe Montana gets on a Sunday. My birthday was coming up and Felicia had a friend edit and transfer the tape to 16mm film. He cut it so that it was just me on the film, and it ran damn near five minutes.

The 14th is a very long par five and it's a dogleg right. Therefore, the cameras behind the tee don't pick you up until your second shot. Jim McKay was the announcer and as I hove into view he said, "And here is actor Jack Lemmon about to hit his second shot." Then there was a long pause and he said, "I beg your pardon, I've just been told he's about to hit his *sixth* shot." I'd managed to put two out of bounds before I reached the corner with my third one.

My amateur partner, who I admire not only for his talent but for his patience, was Jim Garner, a nifty guy and a fine golfer. It was somewhere around the fifteenth or sixteenth when he put his arm and around me and said, "Look at it this way, kid. Yesterday you averaged around 14 or 15 strokes a hole. Today I think you're a shot better."

I have managed to cut out most of the remaining nightmare except for the eighteenth. That was a doozey. I put my first two drives in the water. I put my third one behind the one tree that's in the middle of the fairway. My only choice was to slice it around the tree, so I hit it dead straight into the ocean. I dropped a ball by the sea wall and managed to stay away from the water by hitting it across the fairway and almost into the gallery. To make a long story short, I lay 11 or 12 when I finally reached the green, and I was still about 35 feet from the cup. I was seriously plumb-bobbing the putt. Over my shoulder I said to my caddy, "Which way do you think it'll break?" He said, "Who cares?"

I think it's to my great credit that I still play golf, and I absolutely love it.

Jack Lemmon is a multi-talented artist whose career has ranged from Navy ensign, emcee, actor, pianist, composer, director, and writer for radio, television, theater, film, and fun. Well-educated at eastern prep schools and Harvard, Jack was president of that university's Hasty Pudding Club. Early in his professional life, he appeared on nearly 500 live television performances. He has 48 films to his credit and many awards. Jack has won two Oscars and been nominated 10 more times. Cannes awarded him Best Actor twice, and the British, German, and Canadian Oscars adorn his trophy case. Theater performances have produced one Tony nomination, and an Emmy came from television. If only he could make the cut at the National Pro-am, golfers all over the world would smile and feel relieved.

Ivan Lendl

THE ELEMENTS CONSPIRED AGAINST ME

Spectrum Sports, Inc.

Tennis is my life, but golf and hockey are great loves. I play golf every chance I get—sometimes the same day I play in a tennis tournament. I play backwards—tennis I play righty, but golf I play lefty. This is backwards from how John McEnroe and Martina Navratilova do. They play tennis lefty, but golf righty.

My favorite golf story happened last fall. I was playing golf in the Hartford, Connecticut area with a friend. Going into the last hole, my friend was teeing off and hit the ball into the dead center of the nearby lake. This should have been to my advantage, except the lake was frozen over with ice. The golf ball bounced off of the lake, onto the far side of the fairway, continued to roll, and right onto the green. He then was able to putt and beat me. I felt sure this was incredible luck on his part, but he insisted he did it deliberately.

Ivan Lendl has been one of the top-ranked tennis players in the world for nearly 10 years. He has won eight Grand Slam events, including three U.S. Opens. Ivan has competed in several celebrity golf events.

Nancy Lieberman-Cline

SHANK YOU VERY MUCH

When I was in college, my advisor kept telling me, "Nancy, you've got to play golf. You would be a really great golfer." He loved golf, and I think the older you are, the more you have an appreciation for golf—unless you're young and you've grown up around it. As a child, I was never around golf or tennis. And I was from New York—I never had the patience for that type of game. Finally, though, when I went to the Superstar's Competition in 1979, one of the events that I had to select was golf. I just figured, "It can't be that bad." I started practicing and really enjoyed it. For me the most difficult thing was the embarrassment. I remember going out to the golf range to try and practice before I ever had a lesson. All of these people were around me and I was trying to figure how to hit a golf ball. One time I hit the ball so hard, the golf club slipped out of my hands and flew off and I'm stuck yelling, "Excuse me over there. Could you hold up on that shot?" It was hard not to notice I was the only one running out on the practice tee to get my golf club—which landed farther away than the ball.

After I got a bit better, I played in a tournament down at Hilton Head. There was this real easy hole that had to be a little eight-iron over water—a real short shot. I thought, "No problem," especially as the women's tees were up pretty far. Everybody was pretty impressed with me because I'm an athlete, I'm in shape and I can hit the ball a long way. So, I went to hit the ball—and I shanked it way right. There were these condos to the right. I think the ball went into some guy's living room. I started to worry I'd have to play my second shot from behind his TV. I was already sensitive to feel the embarrassment of the prospect of knocking on someone's door saying, "Excuse me, sir. Could I just move your VCR for a second? And, could you open that sliding glass door, because I really don't want to break it." Of course the tournament committee let me take a drop instead. Immediately I put it right in the water. In fact, it hit a baby alligator.

Nancy Lieberman-Cline is a basketball player extraordinaire. She won a gold medal in the Pan American Games in 1975, a silver medal in the Olympics of 1976, a Broderick Cup and Wade Trophy for her play at Old Dominion. She was also the first woman drafted by a men's professional team. The television voice of women's basketball for NBC at the 1992 Barcelona Olympics and for ESPN/Prime Network's coverage of women's collegiate basketball, Nancy also owns Promotion Events, Inc., a sports marketing company. Her autobiography, *Lady Magic*, has recently been published.

Nancy Lopez

THE OLDER YOU GET

They say the older you get, the more you take things in stride. I'm not so sure.

A few months ago I was playing the Sara Lee Classic in Nashville. At the hotel I rode up the elevator with a couple of high school guys. I knew they were high school guys because the night before they'd had a prom there. While we were all standing there, they looked over at me and saw the endorsements on my bag. One asked, "Are you playing in the golf tournament?" I said yes.

89

They looked me over again, checked out the endorsements on my bag again, and got real excited. I thought they were going to ask me if I was Nancy Lopez. (I get a lot of that.) They kind of bounced up and down all excited and instead one came out with, "Are you Sara Lee?"

I didn't know what to do. I just stood there, shocked. They probably thought I was an idiot.

It's not easy having to deal with getting older and really being a veteran on the tour. I don't want to be older. When that kid asked if I was Sara Lee, I thought, "I am ancient."

Nancy Lopez is one of the most loved great players the LPGA has ever produced. She arrived at the Hall of Fame in 1987 after only 10 years of competition on tour. Her current win record is 43, including four major championships. Nancy and her husband, former baseball great Ray Knight, are the parents of three daughters.

Dave Marr

THE ULTIMATE SAND TRAP

International Management Group

Let's face it. In golf, sand is bad.

Golf course designers deliberately put little pockets of sand all over the place, sometimes for definition and sometimes for challenge. Often, it seems sand is there simply to spoil a perfect round of golf. The architects seems to know in advance where you're going to hit the ball. They've got that sand waiting for you.

I have had many run-ins with sand traps, but the worst

by far came in 1957. I had just bought myself a new little two-door Ford coupe and set off to play the winter tour for the first time. I really thought I was pretty slick in my new car and $1500 in my pocket as a bankroll! In those days you could play for around $250 a week.

I had never driven to the West Coast before. Actually, I had never been farther west than San Antonio, when I left Houston on December 27th to drive to California and play in the Los Angeles Open. I decided that since this was my first trip, I was going to make it a scenic run and enjoy every minute of it. I stopped along the way at all the reptile and alligator farms. I stopped in Tombstone, Arizona and other places I had heard of along Route 66. As I was driving alone, I allowed myself to take as long as I wanted and stop anywhere, just as long as I arrived in Los Angeles in time for the tournament.

The route in California took me through Indio, and I remembered hearing Jimmy Demaret talk a lot about Palm Springs. So off I detoured on the road to Palm Springs in my shiny new car, taking in the sights, thinking extravagant thoughts of playing golf and conquering the world.

I'm zipping along, when out of nowhere a huge sandstorm suddenly appeared. I kept driving as carefully as the very reduced visibility allowed. Other cars were pulling off the road to get some cover, but conditions didn't seem any worse to me than the Texas rainstorms we'd get back home. I did notice that my windshield was very gray and foggy to look through, but I kept going. Pretty soon the sandstorm ended and I picked up speed, determined to make it to Palm Springs in good time.

It turned out I had driven straight through Palm Springs during the storm and didn't know it. I stopped in Beaumont, California, to get some gas. The station attendant came out the way they used to do before self-service, looked at me, looked at my car, and said, "Wow, you've been through a sandstorm!"

"How can you tell?" I asked.

"Come out and look at your car!"

I got out and to this day I will never forget what I saw. The sand had stripped every touch of paint off all the parts of my car. My brand new car looked like it was wrapped in foil.

I drove my poor car to Los Angeles, and had it cleaned and repainted. The sand-pocked windshield also needed to be replaced.

I tied for third in the tournament, and won $1900.

To this day, when I sit around talking to other golfers about the sand traps they have suffered and conquered, I tell them about the ultimate sand trap I once had to play through.

Dave Marr won the 1965 PGA Championship and three other tour events. He was a member of the Ryder Cup team in that same year and captain in 1981. Dave was the golf analyst for ABC-TV's golf coverage for the past 22 years, and now designs golf courses with Jay Riviere.

Johnny Miller

HEARING VOICES

My most interesting story happened in 1973. I had already won a couple of tournaments that year. The press called me a "young lion" and they were expecting me to be one of the next top players with Lanny Wadkins, Grier Jones, Jerry Heard, and Jim Simons. We were all sort jockeying for position and the press liked to write about us. I was playing in the

U.S. Open, which I'd come close to winning a couple of times. I showed up on Monday and played my practice round. I walked off the eighteenth green and a lady came up to me and said, "I predict things. I'm never wrong. You're going to win the Open." Of course I said, "Great! Sounds good to me."

I didn't think much of it, but on Tuesday she was there. After the round she said the same thing. Wednesday, after the round, again she said the same thing.

Wednesday I went in to get my pairing and found I was paired with Arnold Palmer—in Oakmont, Pennsylvania. (Oakmont—there's probably a two-stroke penalty right there.) Arnold Palmer was always bigger than big, but in 1973, in Pennsylvania, he was absolutely huge. But I thought, "What the heck. It'll be an experience playing with Arnold." And besides, that lady was telling me I was going to win.

The first two rounds I shot 71–69. Arnie shot 69–71. We were in third place, a couple of strokes back, and that lady was still there, every day, after each round. On Saturday I went out to play—and forgot my yardage card. In those days you used a local caddy and my local caddy wasn't too knowledgeable. So, I was basically reduced to guessing my yardages. I was five over par after six holes and ended up finishing five over par for the day. I couldn't wait to see that lady because I had blown myself out of the tournament. She never showed.

Everybody who was anybody was on top of the leader board. It was like a Who's Who—Arnold was up there, Jack was up there, Gary Player was up there, and Lee Trevino was one shot out. The whole field was playing well. My best friend

Jerry Heard was also tied for first with Arnold, Jack and Gary, and it looked like he might break through as *the* "young lion."

Sunday I went out to my locker and there was a letter there that said, "You are going to win the U.S. Open." It was postmarked from Iowa and wasn't signed. I thought this was really unusual. I'd never had this kind of thing happen before. I just thought they were wrong.

I went out to the practice tee, and was about to go to the putting green when an inner voice said to me, "Open your stance way up." Then I started thinking to myself that I'd never done that. Why would I want to that now? But I said to myself, "Okay, I'll listen to this voice." So, I opened my stance way up, like Lee Trevino. I hit about five balls and seemed to hit them all right that way. I said to myself, "Okay, I'll try this."

I went out to the putting green and hit a few putts. I went to the first tee and hit a good drive followed by a good five-iron. That's probably the hardest par four in the world, the first hole at Oakmont.

On Sunday, with my yardage card in hand, I birdied the first three holes. On the fourth hole, I almost made an eagle, but settled for my fourth birdie in a row. It wasn't real hard deductive reasoning that if I birdied the first four holes at Oakmont the leaders would all be choking. I figured I'd be about two strokes out of the lead. So, I got really nervous and left a couple of putts short the next two holes and three-putted on 8. The first was from about 18 feet underneath the hole; I left it short, and then missed it.

I got mad at myself for choking. I thought, "You're giving up this chance to win this golf tournament." Well, that sort of spurred me on after almost getting angry at myself after that three-putt. I then birdied 9, parred 10, birdied 11, 12, 13 and 15. I hit every single green—always with an open stance. I made nine birdies that day and my average birdie putt was probably only five or six feet long.

That was my most inspired round of golf, and it seemed to come out of nowhere. The day before I wasn't playing that well, had been struggling all week, but obviously now I had shot a career round—and had a one-shot lead. Arnie was an hour and a half behind me.

As soon as I finished, I felt an inner confirmation that I was going to win. I just knew it—I don't know how, but I knew it. Everyone else still had seven holes of golf left, and I was in a sort of trance. If you've ever seen a picture of me, it's a wild look. You have to see that look to believe it.

Of all the tournaments I've ever played, that one seemed the most "meant to be." A lot of coincidental things occurred: the people pulling for me, the "voice," the letter. . . . Shooting 63 at Oakmont—the hardest course in America—on the final day to win by one stroke, that was pretty exciting.

I never did see or hear from that lady again. But wherever you are, whoever you are, thanks a lot.

Johnny Miller has won 23 PGA tour titles since turning pro in 1969 as well as a number of events throughout other parts of the world. He has competed on two Ryder Cup teams and three World Cup teams. Johnny now works for NBC-TV as the golf color analyst while raising six children.

Anne Murray

WHAT DO YOU USE ON WATER HAZARDS?

Denise Grant

I got started playing golf when I was a kid. Back then, living in Nova Scotia, my five brothers and I spent all of our summers at a place called North Port. When the tide went out, it would go out for about a mile. We'd take our clubs, go out on the sand flats, and hit the balls around. We didn't have a golf course there, so we just depended on the tide.

As we got a little older, we played a bit at a golf course about 20 miles away. But I didn't get really active until I got to university. In phys ed, I took a golf class and now I play as often as I can. Of course, it's never as much as I'd like.

I got to know Sandra Palmer when I did a women in sports show with Perry Como in Lake Tahoe in 1975. Sandra had just won the Dinah Shore. We hit it off at the show, and just kind of kept in touch. I even played in the Dinah Shore in 1976, so I got to know Hollis Stacy, Sandra, and some of the other girls. If I was ever near a tournament, I'd swing by and watch them all play. I'm an avid fan. I'm not a very good player myself. I shoot around 100, but if I took the time and some lessons, I think I could be very good at it. I played Pebble Beach for the first time this year. That was a thrill.

One of my favorite stories, however, happened before my husband and I were married. We were playing golf in Las Vegas and it was the first time he'd ever played. We were on the fifth hole at Dino's, which has a big water hazard. It wasn't a long hole, but there was mostly water between the tee and the green. My husband got up and hit the only six balls he had into the water. By the time he had hit the fifth ball, I was behind a tree laughing, but I didn't dare let him see me hiding.

He immediately hated the game. In fact, he was so mad that he walked right into the water, up to his waist, and started fishing for golf balls. After emerging from the depths, soaked from head to toe, he felt much better, loaded some 20 balls into his bag, opted to skip the fifth hole, and walked straight to the sixth.

Another time, my brother Bruce, who used to sing with me, and I were in Lake Tahoe playing golf with two other musicians. The weather then was getting fairly cold, but we bundled up, and played an entire game behind this older couple. They were a very sweet couple, but the woman wasn't much of a golfer. She'd hit the ball about 20 feet, and play approximately 15 shots per hole. But she was having a good time.

We were very close to them the whole day. At about the fifteenth hole, probably a 75-yard hole, we were so close, we could see everything. On the other side of the green was the lake. The old lady teed off and hit the ball right over the green and into the middle of Lake Tahoe. It was the only solid hit she had had all day. She was so proud of herself. I could hear her husband ask, "Honey, what did you use?" She said something I couldn't catch. All of a sudden this little old man reared back and cried out, "Jesus Christ, you used your f***ing driver!" He was mad as hell and she was pleased as punch.

His voice echoed loudly off of the lake so all of Lake Tahoe heard him. We laughed so hard we couldn't play for three holes. That was about 10 years ago, and our group has been using that line ever since.

Anne Murray has had four platinum albums, four Grammy Awards, three Country Music Awards, three American Music Awards, and 28 Juno Awards. She has hosted four of her own specials on CBS and made numerous other television appearances.

Jim Murray

POEM

Los Angeles Times

Alas! The world is still a testy par five
Over the water with poison ivy in the rough,
An alligator in the sand trap and the pin
Cut over a cliff with the ocean at the
Bottom. The world is an unplayable lie.

This is **Jim Murray**'s first published poem. Jim, is a Pulitzer Prize–winning *Los Angeles Times* sports columnist. He also writes a golf column for *Golf Magazine.*

Leroy Neiman

THE GENERAL PLAYS THROUGH

Paul Chapnick

One of the reasons why my golf career was curtailed goes this way.

I used to golf considerably during my teens before entering the army in World War II. At the war's conclusion, as a G.I. in the Army of Occupation stationed in southern Germany, a fellow enlisted man and I used to play a round several times a week at a Freiburg golf course.

One day, as we were putting on the fourteenth green, a military jeep came bouncing over a rise on the course, then charged down the fairway. An M.P. leaned out of the vehicle and shouted, "Everybody off the course, mach schnell!" Naturally, following orders, we picked up our bags of clubs and hurried off the course army-style.

It turned out that the reason everyone had to clear off the course was that General Patton's threesome was teeing off on the first tee and had to have the whole landscape to themselves for security, eliteness or whatever. No one bothered to explain.

That turned me off and I just never really got back to golf with any consistency except as a truly great subject to paint.

LeRoy Neiman is the foremost sports painter of our time.

Byron Nelson

A PUTTER'S REVENGE

Frank Christian, Jr.

I think that this is my favorite story. After I left the tour, Eddie Lowery, the biggest golf booster I ever saw, called me up. He'd arranged some exhibitions in the San Francisco area, so I went out and played. He usually had me coaching Ken Venturi or Harvie Ward. I didn't get paid for coaching, but the organizers usually paid us $300 just to come out and play.

One day, Eddie called me up and asked me, "Byron, how are you playing?" I told him I was playing all right. This time he pressed, "Are you really playing all right?" And I said, "Yes, I'm playing well, Eddie. Why?" He said, "Well, out at the Santa Rosa Country Club there are two brothers that I've been playing and they're picking me like a chicken. I want to arrange an exhibition up there. You and I will team up and we'll play them, if you're playing good." I was always happy to help a friend being taken, so with conviction I told him I was playing good and would be there as soon as he wanted me.

The game was arranged. On the night before, we went out for dinner in San Francisco. When we came back from dinner, Eddie invited me upstairs. He kept some putters and a putting clock in his bedroom. He found me an old MacGregor center-shafted metal Spur putter he wanted me to use. He didn't think I was a very good putter. I wasn't a bad putter, but I never was a real hot putter like some of the guys are now. Nevertheless, I practiced with him. After we fiddled around with several putters, he said, "Use that one, the Spur." I said, "Oh, no. I don't want to do that." But he insisted. I had no confidence in the putter but if Eddie thought we'd beat the brothers with my using it, I decided to give it a try.

We went out to Santa Rosa the next day. We got on the tee, and Eddie said, "We're gonna play the usual Nassau bet." I chopped around the first few holes. I didn't make any bogeys—had a couple of pars and couple of birdies—and then all of a sudden I started making everything. The putter worked almost as if by magic. Every ball dropped. The brothers pressed (offered side bets). But with my game on, and that putter stroking so perfectly, they soon quit pressing. I think they would have rather not played the last holes if they could have come up with a good enough excuse.

Meantime, Eddie was figuring all the Nassau bets with them. All of my attention was on playing. I had 12 birdies and six pars, for a 60. He got all of his money back. We had great fun. It really was one of the best rounds I've ever played because most of the putts went in and I was 12 under par.

As a reward, Eddie said, "I want you to take that putter and I don't want you to ever use another putter." I took it and used it for about a month. I never made another putt with it.

I gave it back to him and he called me all kinds of names. Then I told him that I must have made all the putts that were in that putter during that one day in Santa Rosa. He laughed and had to agree with me.

Byron Nelson won 52 official PGA tournaments. His name is still prominent in the record book with the most consecutive victories: 11 in 1945; the most wins in one calendar year: 18, again in 1945; and the most consecutive finishes in the money: 113, during the 1940s. Known for his brilliant play, Byron has also been an ambassador for the game throughout the world. He has been the principal mentor to Tom Watson during Tom's success on tour. Byron also shares his convictions about golf through books and the design of many courses.

Jack Nicklaus

IT DEPENDS ON WHAT YOU MEAN BY PRESSURE

Brian D. Morgan

A lot of people have complimented me over the years on handling pressure pretty well. As one of Barbara's and my favorite family stories illustrates, I guess it depends on what you mean by pressure.

Right around the time our first-born, Jackie, was due, shortly after I'd won the 1961 Amateur at Pebble Beach, my Ohio State college coach, Bob Kepler, and I were due to defend a pro-am tournament down in Cincinnati. As it happened, Barbara had already started labor when it was time for

Bob and I to leave our home in Columbus. As is typical of Mrs. Unselfishness, she hadn't told me about it, because she knew I wouldn't go and defend the tournament if I knew, which she thought wouldn't be the right thing to do.

So I gave her a kiss and a "Let me know what's going on, won't you?" and off Bob and I went down to Cincinnati.

The next morning around 8:00 A.M., the phone rings in my hotel room and it's Barbara. "Hi there," I say. "What in the world are you doing calling me so early?"

"Well," says Barbara, "I just thought you ought to know you have a beautiful little boy for a son."

"Oh, gosh," I say, "I'll come right on home."

But Barbara says, "No, don't do that. There's nothing you can do now. Just go play in the tournament, then come home tonight."

So Bob and I go and play our round, then I drive back to Columbus and go straight to the hospital. I walk into where the babies are and I ask the nurses, "Which one of those is mine?"

And one of them says, "That one, over there." And I look around, and there's this great-looking baby, and I say to myself, "Wow, that one's mine," and, *pow,* over I go backwards . . . fainted . . . passed out cold. It's a wonder I didn't crack my head open on that old terrazzo floor.

Well, our next baby is Steve, and this time I'm at the hospital when he's born. After Jackie there's no way our doctor will let me anywhere near the delivery room. But when they finally bring Stevie out I take one look at him, and *pow,* I'm out again, flat down on the floor.

The third time we go to the hospital, it's for Nan. They bring Nan out, and this time they have two people standing there ready to catch me. Sure enough, out I go again, dead to the world. In fact, this time I spend more time in the recovery room than Barbara does.

A couple of years later along comes Gary, and *this* time I'm ready. Really ready. I have smelling salts in my hand, and I'm actually lying down when they bring him in. Not that it helps. Out I go again, absolutely stone cold. In fact, they have to pry the smelling salts out of my hand so they can use them to revive me.

When our last child, Michael, comes along, everyone again spends more time on getting ready for my passing-out than on helping Barbara give birth. Finally, dear old dad does manage to remain conscious through the whole deal.

But oh, the pressure!

Let me tell you that by comparison, going into Amen Corner on a Sunday afternoon in April with a one-stroke lead is an absolute piece of cake.

Named "Player of the Century," **Jack Nicklaus** has taken excellence to a new level. Jack has won 71 regular tour events, including 20 major championships. Since becoming a senior player, his winning ways continue with five victories. Especially sweet was the win at the 1991 U.S. Senior Open, where he shot 65 in a play-off with Chi Chi Rodriguez. Jack has represented the U.S. on eight Ryder Cup teams (twice as Captain), six World Cup teams, and two Walker Cup teams.

Deborah Norville

HIGH STAKES GOLF

Several years ago, when I was living in Chicago, a buddy took me out for a casual date. Included was a round of Goofy Golf. As luck would have it, I was "on" my game that night! I somehow managed to read the Astroturf correctly on hole number three or four and made a hole in one. My friend said, "Bet you can't do that again!" To which I replied, "Oh yeah, what do you wanna bet?" He said, "Name it." So, I suggested he buy me lunch if I made the next hole in one.

I sidled up to the rubber tee-off pad, gripped my putter, and tapped. Once again, the ball rolled squarely past the wooden barricades, banked off the side boards, and plopped right into the cup.

Though he knew he'd have to buy me lunch, my friend was quite sure I couldn't make it three in a row. "Wanna bet?" I asked. "Sure," he said, knowing he'd never have to honor this bet. I said, "Okay. Lunch in the city of my choice!" To my friend's credit, he never flinched. Of course, he was sure my string of luck had ended!

Once again, with the pressure mounting over the magnitude of this putt, I assumed my stance at the head of the putting green, studied the turf, the sideboard, and the obstacles formed by the little concrete mountains built into the hole. I drew the putter back, made contact, followed through—and sank the putt!

At this point my friend blanched and said, "Okay, what city?" I could have chosen any city in the world, because there were no limits placed on the bet. I thought for moment about Paris and London, or some exotic island in the Caribbean . . . and took pity. New York was my choice. True to his word, my friend arranged a plane ticket, booked me a hotel room, and then met me in New York for lunch!

I guess by telling this story publicly I've lost my amateur status. No one is going to try to hustle me on the Goofy Golf Course from now on!

Deborah Norville, host of her own program on ABC Radio, is a former co-host of NBC's "Today Show."

Merlin Olsen

GOLF ON HORSEBACK

Golf has always been a great release for me—a way for me to get away from the things that are grinding me down. Anything that takes me out of doors, out into the sunshine and fresh air, is a very positive thing. And golf is such a humbling game. Even when you think you've got it mastered, it comes right back and bites you.

Early on I was quite a powerful hitter. I remember chipping back to par fours. But I don't do that any more. I've lost all of that length and now I hit sand wedges into greens.

Back in the late 1960s, I was playing in an NFL Player's Tournament at the Canyon Country Club in Palm Springs, California. A lot of people were there from various teams and I was playing ahead of my teammate, Deacon Jones, the great defensive end of the Los Angeles Rams. In those days, Deacon enjoyed having a little nip on the golf course, and on this particular day, he was having a great deal of fun.

As we got to the back nine, he noticed a horse path that runs along the edge of the desert adjacent to the golf course. Several young ladies were riding their horses down this path and Deacon decided, I think, that golf was too slow the old-fashioned way we were playing. What he really seemed to want to do was combine the delicacy of golf with the speed and daring of polo. So he took his golf bag off of the back of the golf cart and talked one of these young ladies into letting him climb onto her horse. This was an interesting idea until the horse either heard the rattle of the golf clubs or suddenly realized that Deacon was 6'5" and weighed around 280 pounds. Deacon had one foot up when the horse took off with Deacon halfway on and halfway off, screaming at the top of his lungs. The horse bounded out across the desert, came to a sudden stop, and Deacon and the clubs went flying in the air out into the cactus and landed in a whole array of beauty.

So ended the polo/golf-playing exploits of Deacon Jones.

Merlin Olsen played NFL football for 15 years, going to the Pro Bowl a record 14 times. He is a member of the College and Pro Football Halls of Fame. Merlin has also spent 15 years as an NFL analyst for both NBC and CBS, besides starring in the TV series "Little House on the Prairie," "Father Murphy" and "Aaron's Way."

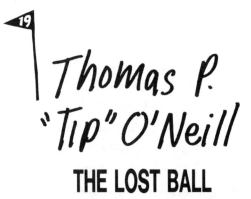

Thomas P. "Tip" O'Neill

THE LOST BALL

It was 1926, and I was a caddy at the Arlmont Country Club, now out of existence. A fellow by the name of George Albright was pro. The caddy master was Freddie Corcoran, who was later to be one of the big men in golf, Ted Williams', Babe Zaharias', and Bing Crosby's manager. Freddie did much for professional golf, men and women.

It was a sunny afternoon in October, and I was caddying for Al Teevens—I remember his name all these years later. On the sixth hole, he sliced a ball into the woods on a long par five. I went in to find the ball. After a little looking I found the ball. One problem: now his clubs were missing. Freddie Corcoran sent several caddies down to help look for the clubs and finally came to the conclusion that someone had stolen them. Six weeks later, after the foliage and leaves had fallen, the clubs appeared hanging from a tree. Apparently, in my haste rushing into the woods to find the ball, I had hung the golf bag on the branch of a tree. I am probably the only caddy in history who found the ball but lost a set of clubs!

Thomas P. "Tip" O'Neill, Jr. has served his country well. He represented his Massachusetts district as congressman for 34 years. "Tip" was also Speaker of the House for 10 years.

Arnold Palmer

THE MASTERS THAT GOT AWAY

    I'm not sure that I would call this my favorite golf story, but it is certainly one that has stuck in my mind these many years because of the lesson that it taught me about over-confidence, about counting my chickens before they hatch. It was one of the greatest disappointments of my career. Golf historians always analyze it when talking about my biggest years in golf, but not in the same way that it lingers with me.

    The subject is the Masters that got away in 1961. From 1958 to 1964 I had some very good fortune in the Masters. I had strong finishes in my first two wins at Augusta National.

(I edged Doug Ford and Fred Hawkins by a stroke in 1958 and came from behind with birdies on the last two holes to nip Ken Venturi by a shot in 1960.) In 1962, I won in a play-off against Gary Player and Dow Finsterwald and in 1964 I won in what certainly was the most consistent and decisive play of the four victories. In two other Masters at that time, Art Wall came up with that amazing finish the last day— five birdies on the last six holes; and Jack Nicklaus outlasted a bunch of others—I wasn't among them—for his first Masters win in 1963. No regrets about those two, but plenty about 1961.

Gary Player was several holes ahead of me in the final round that year. He left the eighteenth green a stroke behind me and I had yet to play the par-five 15th. I didn't birdie there though, and made pars at the 16th and 17th to hold my lead. Then, I hit a very satisfying tee shot at the last hole. As people who follow the Masters closely know, the key to the eighteenth hole at Augusta is getting your drive in a good position off the tee. If you do that with a one-stroke lead, as I did, you are in pretty good shape.

As I approached my ball, I saw an old friend standing at the edge of the gallery. He motioned me over. I was so elated by the situation that I never gave it a thought and walked over to him. He stuck out his hand and said, "Congratulations!" I took his hand and shook it. As soon as I shook his hand, from the moment until I finished the hole, I just knew that I had committed a "no-no." (Later, I remembered how everybody congratulated Ben Hogan for winning his fifth U.S. Open

Championship at the Olympic Club—Gene Sarazen even pronounced the victory on national television—and then Jack Fleck emerged an hour or so later with a tying score. Fleck went on to win the play-off the next day.)

I came off my seven-iron and put the ball in the sand trap to the right of the green. Then I got a little bit greedy and tried to get the ball down where I could make par and still win. Unfortunately I caught it a little thin and put it over the back-left edge of the green, down the slope. I tried to putt the ball back up, but left it 15 feet from the hole. I missed the putt, made six, and lost the Masters.

I tried to put it out of my mind and did to some degree over the years. But you don't ever totally forget a mistake like that. You just learn from it and become determined that you will never do something like that again. Believe me, I haven't in the 30 years since then.

Arnold Palmer has won 61 events on the PGA tour and 92 in all, including seven major championships. Among these are 12 victories on the Senior PGA tour and 19 international titles. As an amateur he won the prestigious U.S. Amateur title. He represented the U.S. on six Ryder Cups, seven World Cups, and on five Chrysler Cup teams. Arnold's far-flung business interests include golf course design worldwide, car dealerships, and other companies.

Gene Perret

SOME MORE BOB HOPE STORIES

Before I ever worked with my boss, Bob Hope, I was a giant fan of his. One of my biggest thrills as a young humor writer was covering a charity pro-am golf tournament he played near my home. Bob played with Arnold Palmer, Doug Sanders and Mike Douglas, whose afternoon talk show was very big at the time.

Mike hit a pitch shot that bit quickly within a foot or two of the cup. Mike was real proud of himself. The big crowd cheered, hooted, and clapped. As Mike strutted up to the green, he passed right in front of Bob, who sneered and said, "Who do you think you are? Merv Griffin?"

Bob is pretty passionate about his golf. And frankly, it's tough for me to come up with golf jokes for him when he's so good at making them up himself.

Once he was playing in a pro-am and he called me about some material that we were working on. I asked him over the phone, "How was your game today?" He replied, "If it was a fight they would have stopped it."

He'd experienced one of his big disappointments in golf. Working on a fairly good round, he'd laid the ball nicely on the final green when his problems started. He told me, "I four-putted the green." I said, "You must have felt terrible." Bob replied, "Not really. They were all long putts."

At the same tournament, Bob was riding in the golf cart and a young lady came running across an adjacent fairway, a baby in her arms. She clutched the infant as she chased Hope's cart, shouting, "Mr. Hope! Mr. Hope!"

When she finally caught up to him, she was almost out of breath. Bob said to her, "What is it, Darling?" While panting she said, "Mr. Hope, I've got to have your autograph." Bob looked at the baby in her arms, looked at her, and said, "Honey, you scared the hell outta me."

When **Gene Perret** was an engineer for General Electric, he wrote and performed humor for retirement dinners and internal functions as a hobby. Phyllis Diller changed his life by discovering him in 1964 in Philadelphia. In 1968 he moved to Hollywood, where his humor has found its way into the routines of Carol Burnett and Bob Hope. Gene has authored three books on using humor for public speaking. He does not play much golf.

Fran Pirozzolo

A GOLF HORROR STORY

Don Sayles

What in the game of golf can possibly match the horror of Frankenstein, the Phantom of the Opera, or Dracula? What terrible tragedy could possibly befall a golfer that could be as horrifying as the animation of Dr. Frankenstein's monster?

To golfers there is a spectre as terrifying as any monster ever created by the pen, one that strikes fear in every golfer's heart. Yes, those most spine-chilling, gut-wrenching of all golf experiences . . . the focal occupational dystonias! The yips!

The yips are a very terrifying brain-behavioral phenomenon that manifest themselves as involuntary movements, usually during putting, although a small percentage of golfers have the yips in chipping, iron play, or driving the golf ball. The involuntary movements can include muscle jerks, twitches, and freezing and are preferentially prominent in the dominant hand and arm. Especially frightening is the fact that the yips don't usually happen on the practice green, but happen just when you fear them most—in tournament play. The yips have ruined many a champion's career. Ben Hogan, Sam Snead, and Tom Watson all have fought the battle of the yips. According to one study, as many as one in four golfers have experienced the yips.

Yippers try a myriad of treatments in order to exorcise the evil demons that cause this dreaded disease. The early interventions are usually changing putters, altering technique or increasing or decreasing practice routines. Next comes the stage of altering visual fixation, separating the hands, putting cross-handed or putting with a long-shafted putter. After that, people try putting with the non-dominant hand, putting while looking at the hole or with the eyes closed. Yippers may resort to hypnosis or prescription drugs for blocking the anxiety and fear at this stage. The terminal phase is marked by divorce, major depression, and a persistent fear that aliens are altering the free radicals in the earth's atmosphere.

Golfers may be surprised to learn that the yips, in one form or another, occur in a wide variety of other sports and even in other non-athletic walks of life and work. "Small muscle athletes," as scientists call them, such as pianists, typists, telegraphers, and writers can become victims of these unusual neuropsychological experiences. Pianists can get an unusual upwards extension of the second and third fingers, or a bizarre flexion of the thumb. Typists, telegraphers, and writers experience painful cramps, tremors and unusual posturing of elbows and hands while practicing their craft.

In baseball the yips have affected many an otherwise great player. The yips manifest themselves during the execution of easy tosses, such as the catcher's throw back to the pitcher and the second baseman's throw to first base. This problem is known in baseball as "Sax attacks" or "Sax disease," after the second baseman Steve Sax, who, while playing for the Dodgers, was crippled by his inability to throw a baseball 40 feet accurately and consistently. In one All-Star game, in front of a huge national television audience, Steve had to make one of these comparatively easy throws; the ball hit the dirt about halfway between second and first, and bounced past the lunge of the first baseman.

The most famous contemporary sufferer of the yips is the great German golfer and Masters champion, Bernhard Langer. His case refutes the theory that "once you've got them, you'll never lose them." It also refutes the theory that older golfers are the most common victims of the disease.

Bernhard has had one major bout of the yips and two

123

minor brushes with them. The first was in 1977, when Bernhard was only 19 years old. During that year's German Open, Langer took over 40 putts per round. A good PGA pro takes 28. On his second hole, he hit his approach shot six feet from the hole. Ten minutes and four putts later, he walked off the green with a double bogey six.

Bernhard described the experience this way: "My putting stroke was a terrible sight. The more I missed, the harder I tried, the worse I got. I expected to miss. I visualized the ball missing. I froze over the ball. My brain just wouldn't instruct my body how to carry out the necessary actions to stroke the putt. I had no backswing at all and the through-swing was just a blurred jab. I felt as though my hands and arms belonged to someone else." Arms and hands that feel like they belong to someone else? Is this the spectre of Dr. Frankenstein's creature, composed of the limbs and parts of another being?

During one bout of the yips Bernhard built up incredible muscle tension. After a round his right arm was rock hard, engorged with blood, looking more like the transplanted arm of Arnold Schwarzenegger.

What caused such a strange physiological effect? A "cumulative workload" factor. A natural human tendency in response to stressful situations is to tense up our muscles—especially those muscles in the face, abdomen, dominant hand and arm. Bernhard recognized this and began paying attention to the need for relaxing his muscles, so they could obey his brain in the act of putting.

Thanks to extraordinary mental toughness and to hundreds of hours of practice and experimentation, Bernhard beat the yips and made himself a champion, good enough to win the Masters and lead the Sony World rankings. In 1991, his peers voted him the best putter in the world.

Mental toughness is the competitive edge that every athlete desires. It enables an athlete to get the most out of every situation—whether he's "got his stuff" or not.

Mental toughness is mental and it's physiological. How well we think dictates how well we feel, which in turn sets off a pattern of physiologic responses in our brain and endocrine system that will help us (in the short and long terms) or send us to the bottom.

When we are faced with a clutch putt, we can react through two physiologic systems. The first such neural system is a pathway between the hypothalmus, an important mechanism deep in the brain, and its connections to the sympathetic nervous system and the adrenal medulla. The sympathetic nervous system mediates the "flight or fight" response—that charge we get that mobilizes or defends, causes the heart-pounding, sweaty-palmed, muscle-bound effects that we have all experienced when we are scared. This is the brain's electrical storm that happens so chronically in yippers.

The second neural system involves the hypothalmus, the pituitary gland (the chief executive of the hormone systems) and the adrenal gland, which pumps adrenaline.

Mentally tough athletes have low baseline levels of activity in both systems. When a challenge arises, the first neural system springs into efficient action. The second system isn't activated. The mentally tough individual does not have a long-lasting, abnormally high arousal level caused by the chronic over-activation of the second neural system. He doesn't collect stress. He doesn't let the "cumulative work-load" overwhelm him.

The physiologic and psychologic reactions of the mentally weak are more exaggerated, pervasive, and longer lasting. There is more unfocused arousal, disorganized thinking, anger, confusion, and excessive muscle tension.

The really scary part is that without mental toughness, this over-activation of the second system causes a cascade of more bad attitudes, more dysfunctional physiologic responses. More bad putts, more fears make horror movies in his mind's eye. The golfer loses his ability to feel positively charged, relaxed, enthusiastic—ready to meet any challenge.

Let me cite a case example of a more typical amateur golfer: one with less talent, less time for practice, etc. The average reader may relate more closely to how he is overcoming the yips. Of course, as a licensed clinical neuropsychologist, I must protect the confidentiality of my patients.

CASE STUDY

The patient is a 67-year-old male who is in excellent health. Recent medical history includes only a single incident of atrial fibrillation while jogging. Current medications include radioisotope treatment of Graves' disease. Recent stressors include the patient's job stress: he is chief executive officer of a large concern. The past year has been especially stressful at work since the organization he represents entered into a conflict in the Middle East over oil and gas rights, among other issues. His successful management of the matter revealed that he is at his best under pressure. It is unclear at this time why he cannot transfer these acquired occupational skills into the athletic arena, where, as a middle-handicap golfer, he reports difficulties with putting.

The first recommendation for this golfer was to increase his trust in a sound method. I sent him a list of several mental and physical practice routines that he could use to overcome the yips. I also sent him a training device (known as ON-TRAC) to improve his stroke. A better technique never hurt any golfer! This training technique and the exercises were ones that he could do at home for a few minutes a day. And finally, as mentioned above, this fellow, a Texan, is known for his mental toughness. He speaks in public and to the media often, always giving confident self-projections. The challenge then becomes one of transferring his mental toughness, with appropriate levels of relaxed self-regulation, to the golf course.

Actually, the subject of my case study has come upon another solution to his yips. His golfing partners regularly concede putts inside 10 feet. Of course, what works for the President of the United States might not work for you.

Dr. Fran Pirozzolo is one of the country's leading sports scientists. His recent research work for the National Research Council and National Academy of Science's book publication, *In The Mind's Eye,* provides basis for and insight into what works and what doesn't work for human performance enhancement. He consults with numerous elite athletes and teams. Dr. Pirozzolo, Chief of the Neuropsychology Service at Baylor College of Medicine, is a frequent speaker at golf and other sports educational workshops. He has written numerous articles on performance enhancement for all levels and interests.

Gary Player

A DESPERATE SHOT

As a young professional golfer in South Africa, I dreamed about going to play in Great Britain. I saved my money giving lessons. In those days I earned one dollar a lesson, which I split fifty-fifty with my boss. Most days I would give 20 lessons. Teaching others proved a good education for me.

During my first trip to Britain in 1955, I played in a tournament in Leeds. I was playing well and got to the last hole, a par five, and felt that a birdie would win the tourney for me. I hit a good drive down the middle and decided to use my driver on the second shot as well in order to reach the green in two. Unfortunately, I hooked this shot and it went right up against a stone wall that stood to the left of the green. It was one of those old English walls, made of rugged stone.

The way the ball nestled right next to it, I saw I had no chance to chip it back. But I knew what I had to do. "I'll knock the ball against the wall and it will ricochet back onto the green," I said to myself.

I took a hit at the ball—but it ricocheted and hit me on the jaw. Knocked me right out!

I lay on the ground for a few seconds, stunned. But the desire to win gripped me. Quickly I got up and chipped onto the green. Now I've played four! All I need is a 20-foot putt for par, and I can probably escape with a tie for the lead.

I was still dazed. I really and truly saw two holes. Nevertheless, I putted, and the ball found the real hole. What a par! I was very pleased.

However, I soon learned that because I had allowed the ball to touch me, I had incurred a two-stroke penalty. I lost the tournament by a single stroke.

That tournament meant a lot to me. The members of my club in Johannesburg had collected money for me. My father, a poor man who worked in the gold mines, had given me a new set of clubs, and I only found out later that he had to get an overdraft to buy them. I needed the money.

I left home with two pairs of pants, both too large for me. I pulled them up with a belt and wore a sweater to cover that up. The news media criticized me for looking untidy. Little did they realize that I simply could not afford new clothes.

Boardinghouses could be found for seventeen and sixpence, providing bed and breakfast. We traveled by train and bus and trams. There was no such thing as courtesy cars. That first year I traveled with three other young South Africans.

It was tough but character-building, to say the least. I still appreciate today every check I receive, every contract I sign; I am truly grateful for my success and all its rewards. I remember the desperation of those days—and I'm glad to say that all that has stayed is the desperation to win.

Gary Player has set a standard of sharing himself with the world of golf, traveling more miles than any other modern player. He also has set standards of play in major championships as a younger man and as a senior player. Gary has won all four majors on both tours. All told, he has won 73 tournaments. He was inducted into the World Golf Hall of Fame in 1974.

Judy Rankin

RON MULLINS, CADDY EXTRAORDINAIRE

Capital Cities, ABC, Inc.

One of the things you hear from golfers at all levels is how many wonderful people you meet through golf. Me, too. I met one of the most charming characters I'm sure I will ever know on the links.

Back in the 1970s, the LPGA played the Colgate European Open outside of London at a wonderful club called Sunningdale. It was a totally natural golf course; all they did was mow the right places. I guess I've gotten more enjoyment and love out of the game of golf on that course then anywhere else.

They've since put in a sprinkler system to water the greens. But back then, the course was more manicured by nature and time than anything else and you got to play the old style of golf. When a golf course is weathered by time, you may want to hit the ball on the right side of the green to get it to the left side. The green may be so firm that you can't fly the ball onto the green no matter how skilled you are. In America, we don't see a lot of golf like that. Our courses have a tendency to be over-manicured.

In order to play well on a natural course, you have to either know the course like the back of your hand, or you have to have a caddy who does. I was lucky enough to get one of the very best caddies at Sunningdale.

The gentleman's name was Ron Mullins. He was about 5'6", not a big man, but really put together, especially for someone in his sixties. Graying brown hair, not all of it still on his head. He enjoyed a pint after the round, but kept himself in remarkably good shape for a man his age. He always wore a coat and tie.

He called me "Madame." I called him "Mull." We would make our way around the golf course with me executing the shots, and in most cases, him executing the plan. Mull was quite a legend in the area, having worked that piece of ground for about 50 years. He had been caddying at Sunningdale since he was 13 years old.

David Foster, the chairman of Colgate, and Graham Lockey were members of Sunningdale, and had been playing there months before. David was responsible for the tournament coming to Sunningdale, and Mullins went over to them and asked whom he should caddy for. They said, "You ought to get Judy Rankin. She might have a good chance here." That's how it came about, and I'm forever grateful.

I had played in the British Amateur when I was 16 years old—and did not fare well. The American style of "air golf" I had grown up with just didn't work on the Scottish course. There you had to play the bounces in order to succeed, and when I showed up at Sunningdale in 1974—the first time I took on a British course since the earlier disappointment—I was not convinced that I could make the adjustment. True, I had been playing well in recent tournaments, but when you go to another country, you lose your identity a little bit. You think that the local caddies or pros must be more knowledge-able than you are. In this case, it was absolutely true: Ron Mullins did know more than I ever would about Sunningdale.

During a practice round, before the tournament ever started, we were at the fifth hole—a pretty interesting, beautiful par four. I drove from the high tee . . . and had my first heather experience. We walked to where my shot had landed, he set the bag down (he never used a cart to carry the golf bag, as other caddies did), and I guessed that I probably couldn't get the ball onto the green. There was water to the right, so I reached for my seven-iron. He put his hand on the seven-iron and pushed it back into the bag. With his other hand, he offered me my sand wedge. "Madame," he said. He didn't even discuss it with me.

I hardly knew the man at this point, but I knew I had a

formidable force here. I ripped at the ball as hard as I could with the wedge and moved it out of the heather about 20 yards. Evidently, he knew what I needed.

I was in the lead when we came to the fourteenth hole, a par three, during the last round of the tournament. I hit a pretty good shot to the green, about 10 feet short of the hole. Mull always read the putts. He was very good at that. He said, "Left edge of the hole." I looked at this putt, and had looked at a couple of putts in my life before that, and said, "Mull, don't you think it breaks a little more than that?"

"No, Madame. Left edge of the hole."

Well, I putted, and missed by about two or three inches to the right of the hole. As we walked off the green, I said, "Mull, I think that putt broke a little more than you thought."

"It did not, Madame," he said. "You shanked it."

I never argued with him again.

Mull was the captain of our ship. The one thing he wasn't too big on was exact distance. I would ask, "How far is it?" and he'd approximate, "Oh, it's about. . . ." I'd be out there stepping off yardage and trying to be very exact, and he'd pull out his handkerchief and hold it up to check the wind. I'd think there wasn't a breath of wind blowing, and he'd have the handkerchief up in the air and say, "The wind is at your back, Madame. I think you'd better hit a little less club." He was just about never wrong. The man was amazing.

I can honestly say that he knew every bounce the ball would take. If he told you to hit the ball there, because it would then go there and there, you could count on it that if you put the ball the first place he told you, it would either go in the hole or leave you a short putt away.

I won the event that year, and won again in 1977. The British papers had quite a time of it trying to figure out just how much of a factor Mullins was. He had such a great reputation. Betting on golf tournaments is legal in England and Mullins' presence was figured in by the oddsmakers.

I'm sure that a good bit of Mull's advice was based on what he knew I could do. At that time, I was a pretty good driver. Because of Mull's familiarity with the course, I felt like I was playing on a course I knew well and could really let things rip. He was very complimentary towards me and my game (except that particular putt which he accused me of shanking). He once told a newspaper reporter that I was the greatest wooden club player that he'd ever seen. That, I thought, was a terrific compliment.

I loved him, my husband loved him. I looked forward to seeing him year after year.

Judy Rankin won 29 tournaments between 1968 and 1979. Judy has been the LPGA's Player of the Year and three times won the coveted Vare Trophy, for the lowest yearly scoring average. Chronic back trouble resulted in surgery in 1985, which curtailed her playing career. Judy provides crisp, clear analysis for ABC's men's and women's golf tournaments. She is in the Texas Golf Hall of Fame.

Fred Raphael

THE SENIOR PGA TOUR

In 1992, the Senior PGA Tour has scheduled some 42 tournaments world-wide with total purses to exceed $23,000,000. Every event will offer a minimum of $325,000 in prize money and 24 of these events will be seen on television.

The credit for the success of the Senior PGA Tour goes to the senior players themselves and the skillful management of Commissioner Deane Beman and his staff as well as to the sponsors who were willing to support the Tour.

But the Senior PGA Tour had its beginning in 1978 in Austin, Texas, with a tournament known as "The Legends of Golf." Little did Jimmy Demaret, Gene Sarazen, a host of other legends, or I realize what we were creating for professional golfers over 50 when we held our first tournament on the NBC network. To put it in golf vernacular, what we were doing was giving all these golfers a well-deserved "mulligan" for the rest of their lives.

How did it all start? You have to go back to the 1963 Masters in Augusta, Georgia. I was having dinner with Gene Sarazen. I asked the Squire what time he was teeing off on Saturday and who he was playing with. As he was unsure, he got up and called the clubhouse. When he returned to the table, he had a great big grin on his face. He said, "Tomorrow, the old legend, Gene Sarazen, tees off with the future legend, Arnold Palmer."

That offhand remark triggered an idea in my mind. But I was busily engaged in producing "Shell's Wonderful World of Golf," which still had another seven years of life in it. Those seven years not only gave me time to mull the idea over and refine it in my mind, but also time to seek the counsel of two people who would become my first two invitees—Jimmy Demaret and Gene Sarazen.

Both were very encouraging. Gene was adamant about who should be invited. He insisted that it only be winners of the PGA, British Open, U.S. Open, and the Masters. Jimmy, on the other hand, saw this more as his own personal "clambake," and wanted more of his golfing pals included. We eventually compromised to include members of the Ryder Cup and the World Cup teams. A few years later, when I wasn't paying attention, Jimmy slipped one past me and invited some winners of the Canadian Open; here came his long-time pal, George Fazio. Not that Fazio didn't belong; after all, his contributions to golf course architecture made him a legend. But that was Jimmy: never forget an old pal. But I'm getting ahead of myself. . . .

In 1970, much to my regret and that of many others in the television viewing audience, the Shell series went off the air. With the encouragement of NBC and then Commissioner of Golf Joe Dey, I tried to find another sponsor. However, every time I came close to one, the potential advertiser and I had to agree that regardless of how many changes we made in the format, the show would always come out looking like "Shell's Wonderful World of Golf." After a couple of years, I gave up and turned my thoughts to that other idea Jimmy and I had talked about so much, The Legends of Golf.

I talked with all three networks, and found little or no advertiser or broadcast interest. "Who would want to watch a bunch of old men who probably can't play the game anymore?" was the constant complaint.

I went on to other projects. But a couple of years later, again due to a visit I had with Jimmy at the Champions, I started to get excited about the concept again. Once more I pursued the networks. At CBS and ABC it was still no dice, but at NBC there was a spark of interest. Mike Trager, then Vice-President of Sports Programming, was looking for something new, something distinctive. A golf addict himself, he found something exciting and unique about the Legends. He went to his boss, Don Ohlmeyer, and pitched the idea to him. Don asked if I could really deliver the players I was talking about. I told him that I already had commitments from all of them. Don felt people could relate to all these players—golfers many in the TV audience had grown up watching and rooting for—and gave Mike the green light. We now had a television commitment. However, that was only half the battle. We still had a couple of other things to iron out: the format and the prize money.

My original format was for a series of seven shows using the best-ball, two-man-team format, to be taped or filmed. Not live—no way was I going to show one of my Legends shanking a shot. But on this point NBC was firm: it would be a live television show on a Saturday and Sunday, or no show at all. Well, I had some soul-searching to do.

Back I went to Jimmy, seeking his opinion—since he was a legend himself—as to whether he thought the players would go along with it. He said, "Fred, go for it." So I did, and signed the contract with NBC.

Now, all I needed was the $400,000 in prize money. It would be golf's largest purse ever. Nobody thought I could deliver. (I must confess, I had a few doubts myself.) A lot of it depended on how well the program would sell. Finally, late that summer, I found a sponsor who seemed most anxious to put up the prize money and I could relax . . . I thought. But in December of that same year, my sponsor dropped out. I was left holding the bag—an empty one. I was in total shock.

I went to NBC, and after much discussion, they agreed to loan the money I would need to arrive at $400,000. As I recall, the pro-am sales amounted to a little over $100,000. So, here I was starting a new venture $300,000 in the red.

Much before that time, I had asked Jimmy where he thought we should play the event, thinking he would say the Champions in Houston. But Jimmy had no intention of bringing a second event into Houston to compete with his friends at the Houston Golf Association, sponsors of the PGA tour event there. He suggested the Onion Creek Club in Austin, Texas. He pointed out that Austin, a growing city, offered the right climate, no spring sports competition, and a course that was made for the senior players. I agreed; anyway, this was an area in which I would not disagree with a Legend, even if I were inclined to do so.

We were about as set as could be. The last week in April arrived and I headed for Austin. What I found was everything Jimmy had said. The climate was perfect. The club members got so caught up in the spirit of the Legends that during tournament week they wore knickers, just as the old legends did in those early years of golf in this country. To top it all, the course itself was just perfect for the older guys.

Finally, it was tournament time and boy, were the players uptight! It suddenly hit them: NETWORK TELEVISION! Would their game hold up? To say they were nervous would be the understatement of all time. A couple of them came up to me and asked if I really had $400,000 in prize money for them. I told them they could check the local bank, but please not before Friday; that's when NBC was to deposit the cashier's check in my name.

But on Sunday, the last day of the three-day tournament, there was no uncertainty about one of the all-time Legends, Sam Snead. He absolutely sparkled on the back nine and birdied 16 to keep him and his partner, Gardner Dickinson, one stroke behind the leaders, Peter Thomson and Kel Nagle. Then on 17 he birdied again and the teams were all tied up going into the final hole. The excitement was electric.

On 18, Sam did it again! His 90-yard wedge shot from the fairway in front of the elevated green was as pretty a shot as Sam ever played, leaving himself just three feet from the cup. After Thomson and Nagle had missed their try for birdies, Sam, with his unique putting style (which Demaret once said, "looks like he's basting a turkey") sunk his putt and won the first prize of $100,000. That was the most money they had ever won in a single golf event, and Sam was now 66 years old and Gardner 50!

Noted golf columnist Dan Jenkins, then writing for *Sports Illustrated,* called it the stuff of legends as he wrote: "At first it was like packing up a golf museum and taking it on the road, in case a lot of folks out there thought Arnold Palmer had invented the game and then lost it to Jack Nicklaus at one of those places like Pensacola or Pinehurst. If so, the Legends of Golf tournament would show them different. Ben Hogan's white cap and cigarette might be missing but on display would be such treasured relics as Gene Sarazen's knickers, Sam

Snead's straw hat, Tommy Bolt's chin, Jimmy Demaret's wit, Cary Middlecoff's dental drill and all sorts of memorabilia from the sport that gave us beltless slacks, and three-toned shoes. As such, it was the best of ideas for a game with so much sameness on the professional tour . . . week after week of wondering who Lou Hinkle is."

With the first year behind us, I looked forward to 1979. Once more I headed for Texas and the second year of the Legends of Golf. Still, without a sponsor, I was short $200,000 in prize money. This time my "angel" turned out to be Onion Creek Club itself. So, after two years, this great idea of mine had me about a half million dollars in the red.

I'll never forget that Saturday night and Sunday morning in April. In all my years, I've never seen such rain. NBC's producer, Larry Cirillo, the Onion Creek staff, and I huddled in the pro shop as we saw my dream of a televised Sunday finish going down the drain in that unbelievable storm. I was so sure we wouldn't play that day, I sent my wife back to New York on an early afternoon flight . . . and she missed the greatest play-off ever.

Miraculously, around 10:00 A.M. Sunday morning, the rain started to lessen, and the ground crew went to work. We pushed our starting times back at least an hour and then as the tournament progressed, watched another miracle take place on the golf course.

Our leading team in the clubhouse after 18 holes was Tommy Bolt and Art Wall, Jr. But when Julius Boros, the nonchalant one, birdied 18, he and partner Roberto DeVicenzo tied the tournament and our two teams went off to 15 to start an unforgettable play-off. After pars on that hole we watched golf history in the making, as both teams birdied the next four holes. It was Wall a birdie, Roberto a birdie, Bolt a birdie, Roberto another birdie. Then still another birdie by Bolt, who pointed his finger towards his opponent with a "Take that!" On the very next hole, a smiling DeVicenzo birdied again and gestured back at Tommy with a "Gotcha!" Finally, on the sixth extra play-off hole, DeVicenzo birdied yet again and it was all over.

That same week Dick Taylor, editor of *Golf World,* described what he witnessed at the Legends that memorable day. "Go on, you mean you didn't see it? You missed that shootout in Texas? What were you watching on TV, arm wrestling from Grenoble, hockey putts, or first man down court shoots, or what? Not the Legends of Golf? Well, if you have a minute or so, I'll try to tell you what happened, but it might defy description. I mean the TV folks were speechless at times over what happened. What it was, was one of the greatest golf shows on earth."

Almost overlooked in the excitement of the play-off was the fact that on Saturday, the legendary Gene Sarazen, then 79, and playing partner Bob Goalby thrilled the national television audience when the scoreboard showed them in second place trailing the leaders by one shot after 12 holes on that next-to-last round of play.

When the dust settled, we realized that dinner plans on the East Coast had been delayed. NBC's nightly 6:00 and

7:00 news broadcast had been canceled. Little did we realize it at the time, but April 30, 1979, was the day the Senior PGA Tour was born. The tour became the sport of the 1980s. And, as a result of that fantastic finish, I found myself a sponsor, the Liberty Mutual Insurance Company. Liberty Mutual has been with the Legends since 1980, and to my great relief the contract with them extends through the year 2001.

LOCKER ROOM QUOTES FROM THE LEGENDS

What do I remember most about the Legends? Well, back in 1978, the initial year of the event, Mike Souchak suggested I get a recording machine and put it in the locker room. "The golf is one thing," he said, "but what really makes this tournament fun is all the needling and funny stories the guys tell in that locker room."

I never realized how right Mike was. While I was never able to record everything that happened over the years in that "restricted area," I'd like to share with you some of the more memorable quotes, some of the fun, and the camaraderie one could only find among these old friends, the Legends.

QUOTES

Gene Sarazen: "One day I was taking flying lessons down in Miami and I noticed that when I pulled the stick back the tail went down and the plane took off. Something flashed in my mind and I said if I did that to a niblick (they didn't call it a sand wedge in those days), it would have the same reaction in a sand trap. I figured the flange would hit the sand and bounce out. You know, in those days I was terrible at getting out of a sand trap. I'd always get a hole where I'd chalk up a 7 or 8. So, I couldn't get out of that plane quick enough. I wired Wilson and asked them to send me a dozen niblicks and I bought all the solder they had in town. I bought rasps and files and then I went out to a little nine-hole course by myself for about two months. When I got through working on my niblick there, I knew I could get down in two every time. Well, I kept that club hidden. I was now ready for the British Open and when I went over to play in the Open I never left that club in the bag. I'd put it under my coat and take it to my bedroom. When the Open started, I was in three traps on the first nine and each time I came out about a foot or two from the hole. All of a sudden, the crowd was saying, 'I say, have you seen that new weapon of Sarazen's?' Well, then it was too late to borrow it and I won the Open hands down. In fact, at one time I was leading by nine strokes and I wound up winning by five.''

Tommy Bolt: "I've been told that my putter had more air time than Lindbergh and I guess that's right. When I let it fly everyone knew 'ole Tom' was around. But I remember Ky Lafoon once had a bad week with his putter and he told me he tied it to the rear of his car and dragged it all the way to the next tournament. . . . It was nothing serious; he just wanted to punish it a little."

Gene Sarazen: "I can't believe we're playing for all this money: $400,000! In 1932, when I won *both* the U.S. Open and the British Open, I got less than $1,000 for winning both major championships. Then in 1935, I got $750 when I got my double-eagle in winning the Masters in a play-off with Craig Wood. True, Craig and I each got an additional $50 for playing the extra 36 holes in that play-off."

Jimmy Demaret: "Well, when I won the Masters in 1940 I got a check for $900. Believe it or not, in 1977, just for showing at the *luncheon* they gave me a $1,000."

Paul Runyan: "In 1934, I was the leading money winner with a grand total of $7,005!"

"Lighthorse" Harry Cooper: "Heck, I was leading money winner in 1937, winning seven tournaments, plus two with Horton Smith as my partner, for a total of $14,138. They get more than that for finishing tenth today. Of course, we didn't pay taxes in those days."

Sam Snead: "Before I became a pro I used to be a soda jerk in my hometown just outside of White Sulphur Springs, West Virginia, and the Doc who owned the shop would go out and look around and as long as one person was on the street, he wouldn't close up. We didn't have any traffic lights in my town.

As a matter of fact, we only had one stop street. Well, nothing in my hometown has ever changed, so years later, when Jimmy Demaret came up to play an exhibition with me he arrived on a weekend. So Jimmy says, 'Hey Sam, it's Saturday night, what's the action around here?' I said, 'Well Jimmy, we can go down and watch 'em get a couple of haircuts!' "

Ralph Gudahl: "Let's face it, old golfers don't fade away, we just lose our distance."

Tommy Bolt: "I'll tell you guys one thing, they've never made as many clubs as I've been accused of throwing. You know, I never threw them very far. I guess in the back of my mind I knew I really wanted to retrieve them."

Ralph Gudahl: "Tommy Bolt threw clubs and got a mean reputation. Bob Jones threw clubs and he became immortal."

Bob Hope: "Some of these Legends have been around golf a long time. When they mention a good grip, they're talking about their dentures."

Jay Hebert: "Would you believe, I had my first hole-in-one in San Antonio on the tenth hole on a Saturday. Then, the next day, I had a second hole-in-one on the fourth hole. I got so nervous I three-putted the next two holes on both days and lost the tournament. Can you imagine getting two aces in one tournament and losing?"

Jackie Burke: "I guess what I remember most about four straight tournament wins was that up to that point I had been putting rather poorly. That first week of the streak I saw Jay Hebert using an old Otie Chrisman putter. I borrowed it, fiddled around with it for a while, and finally decided to use it, and won the tournament. I won again the next week. Then I beat Tommy Bolt in a play-off and won again in St. Pete for four straight—all with a borrowed putter."

Tommy Bolt: "Jackie Burke could make that putter do the damnedest things. He once putted a ball off a bridge. He could make that ball hop puddles of water and anything else that might be in his way."

Jackie Burke: "Let me tell you what happened to that putter. Otie borrowed it from me and took it to his workshop to make a copy of it and would you believe, he broke it while working on it. I almost broke his neck and I haven't putted well since."

"Lighthorse" Harry Cooper: "Jackie, I remember back in the St. Paul Open, I believe it was 1937, I had, would you believe, seven putters on the practice green and I couldn't make up my mind which one to use. I finally rushed into the golf shop to see what I could find. Just as I got into the shop, I heard them calling me to the first tee. I looked down at the bench and saw an old putter head laying there and up above on a rack I saw a raw shaft in the bin. So, I took the shaft down and tapped it into the clubhead and went out and won the tournament with it."

Mike Souchak: "When I started playing, I could hit the ball a ton. Chick Harbert was long, too, and every Wednesday

149

we'd get together, all the boys. First, we'd have a clinic and then put on a driving contest. Heck, I'd pick up a hundred or hundred and a half, enough to pay for my room and caddy fee. Then big George Bayer came along and all bets were off. He made us look like a bunch of 'singles' hitters."

Jimmy Demaret: "After a round at the Legends a friend asked me how I played. I said I made 10 the hard way. I'd been out with Phil Harris till 5:00 A.M. two nights straight."

Sam Snead: "The kids on the tour today are too good losers. Show me a 'good loser' and I'll show you a 'seldom winner.' "

Ken Venturi: "As a youth, I stuttered a lot and the doctor told my mother it was incurable. Well, I couldn't buy that. So, I took up golf and because it's such a lonely game, I started practicing making speeches when I'd go out and hit golf balls. I'd tell myself, out loud, what a lovely shot that was, etc. People used to look at me and wonder who the hell I was talking to, but I didn't care. And when I'd get to the eighteenth hole I'd make a speech as if I has just won the tournament and was accepting my trophy. Well, the funny part of all this was that the first ball I ever hit was at Harding Park where I spent hours trying to improve my game—and my speech as well. And it was at Harding Park that I won my last tournament. When I received my trophy that day on the eighteenth green, I made the same speech I had made on that green a thousand times beginning when I was 14 years old."

"Lighthorse" Harry Cooper: "It was at the Los Angeles Open in 1926 that Damon Runyon pinned the nickname 'Lighthorse' on me. It was the first tournament he ever covered. Since I was leading, he decided to follow me around on that last day. I remember I was playing George Von Elm. In those days I did everything quickly. I walked fast and played just as fast. It took just 2½ hours to play the 18 holes. After it was over and I had won, Runyon came over to me and said that he felt as though he should have been on a horse in order to keep up with me. So, in his newspaper story the next day he referred to me as 'Lighthorse' Harry Cooper and the name stayed with me throughout my career."

Jimmy Demaret: "I always enjoyed myself at night when I played. I've been asked if I could have won more tournaments if I had taken myself and my game more seriously. But I don't know. I was relaxed. I'm relaxed now, even though I've got the shakes a little. As a result, maybe I wouldn't have won more than I did. I do know there were a couple of times when I was leading a tournament and had to drop out on the last day because I was suffering from a terrible hangover. But we all had a great time and I wouldn't change a minute of it."

Roberto De Vincenzo: "When I made all those birdies in the play-off in 1979, my caddy, he say to me, 'Roberto, you only putt good when you are on the television camera, because on the other holes, you putt lousy.' "

Sam Snead: "I quit the PGA Tour because the young guys ran me out. Now, Palmer, January, Miller Barber, and the rest are running me out of the Seniors. I wonder what Raphael has in mind for us guys over 70."

Bob Hope: "Some of these guys are getting on. They still consider it a thrill to play with a ball with dimples on it. In fact, with some of them, it's the only thing with dimples that still thrills them."

"One of the Legends took a five on a hole and marked down a Roman numeral V. Another guy hit a ball 50 yards . . . and that's not bad with a cane."

Ralph Gudahl: "Bob Jones was a fabulous competitor. As an amateur you had to understand that he had tremendous pressure on him playing against those professionals all the time. And you know, even though he was beating all of us, we loved him because he was such a great sportsman and a tremendous credit to golf. I guess his Masters tournament, which was really Bob's creation, says it all . . . *real class!*"

Bob Toski: "It's surprising, but there's really not that much difference in golf instruction today from when I started years ago. Today, there's more emphasis perhaps on arm and leg control, and I guess the biggest change is the grip. Back in the early days we were hands and wrist players. Today, there's more arm and leg players."

Bob Goalby: "Winning the Masters the way I did was unfortunate, not only for me but for Roberto as well. I never did get the full credit I deserved but I had to feel badly for Roberto as well. He was 45 and it was his birthday. However, Roberto told me he probably got as much publicity as I did by his signing an incorrect scorecard."

Roberto De Vincenzo: "Only in America can I sign a wrong card and become a national hero. In my country they would run me out of town for doing such a stupid thing."

Cary Middlecoff: "I'm sitting here with three men, Sarazen, Demaret, and Souchak, and there's got to be a decade, possibly more between them and me and yet each helped me on the tour. When I was playing in the North-South Open, Gene saw me play and was nice enough to recommend me to a sporting goods sponsor, who turned out to be very good to me for many years. Jimmy was the greatest at helping all of us, getting money for guys when they needed it to keep going. And when I became Chairman of the Tour Committee, I remember we had a meeting one night and about 300 members attended. I was having a very difficult time trying to get my point across on a particular subject and a newcomer, Mike Souchak, a very physical All-American football player out of Duke, came to my rescue. Mike listened to the questions being fired at me and at one point quietly walked to the front of the room and said, 'Anybody who has one more derogatory word to say about what this man is trying to do for us and to what he's got to say, has got to try me on for size.' I had no more trouble after that and instantly installed Mike as my Sergeant-at-arms."

Billy Casper: "I had developed some bad habits in golf so that when I became 50 I needed to get my game in shape to play in the seniors. I worked with Phil Rodgers, who did so much to help me, but I also sought out a hypnotist—in fact, two of them—and used the power of 'positive affirmation.' I worked with them for about six months. While under hypnosis and fully conscious I looked at films of myself. We looked at my big wins at the 1966 U.S. Open and the 1970 Masters and took all the positive things that happened in those tournaments . . . whether it was a good putt, a great chip shot, a good swing, a good iron shot or a good sand shot . . . and spliced them together to come up with about 12 minutes of tape which I would watch over and over. What's so fascinating to me about it is that the Russian athletes have been using this same system for many years and for every hour of physical practice, they put in about three hours of this 'positive affirmation.' So, if you tell yourself often enough that you can do it, you will. It worked for me. It's really the power of positive thinking."

Charlie Sifford: "In 1946 we had our own Negro league; we weren't allowed in the PGA then. We had tournaments in Detroit, Chicago, Philadelphia and New York, and at the end of the season we used to have a Negro National Open. First prize was about a thousand dollars. Of course, you didn't need much money in those days. But at least I always had enough to buy my cigars. I've been smoking these things for about 40 years now. But sometimes I'll play an entire round with the cigar in my mouth and never light it up. Of course, if I didn't have it in my mouth, people would say, 'Hey, Charlie, where's the cigar?' People on the course know and recognize me by my cigar. Funny thing about it was that, in all these years, I never got an endorsement from a cigar company to do an ad or a television commercial. . . .''

Doug Ford: ''When I started in golf Italians never seemed to get beyond being caddies or bag boys. There must have been a prejudice toward us. The Scottish were firmly entrenched in the top club jobs. So, we started changing our names. We went from Fortunato to Ford, Saracine to Sarazen. And now, I live like the millionaires I used to caddy for—seven months in Florida and five in Westchester!''

Gene Sarazen: ''There's no doubt in my mind that the players today are so much superior to the players in the 1920s. I began to see the change when those Texas boys, Hogan, Nelson, Demaret, and then Snead came along. After that the crop got better. I'm sure the better-conditioned courses, air travel, and the improvement in the equipment had something to do with it, but I also think the players today have much better swings.''

Jimmy Demaret: ''I truly believe that we had some very fine shot-makers in the early days. Of course, the big advantage the boys have today is that they learn what it's all about in college where they play 20 or 30 tournaments a year and then they have the advantage of an instructor who helps them with their game. You must remember I started with two clubs, a wedge and a nine-iron. I played just about everything with a nine-iron. Then I picked up a five-iron. I trained myself to play four or five different shots with that iron. I wish I could have had an opportunity to learn the game from an Armour or a Hagen.''

Jerry Barber: "I once said to a fellow I was giving a lesson to that people who take lessons don't know what they're trying to do nor how they're trying to do it. And he said, 'Mr. Barber, I'm not paying you to be insulted.'"

Bob Hope: "Well, that's life. The older you get, the tougher it is to score."

Fred Raphael has been one of the giants behind the scenes in golf. Although his own game is suspect, he has brought us golf's first global travelogue and competitive series, "Shell's Wonderful World of Golf," which aired on NBC for nearly a decade.

Betsy Rawls

IMPERFECT PRACTICE

I started playing golf when I was 17 years old. My first tournament was in 1946, the Texas Women's Open at Colonial Country Club in Fort Worth, Texas, and I didn't know much. I had never even seen a big tournament before. I had played in a little event in West Texas and that had been the only tournament golf I had been exposed to.

My father had entered me in the tournament, so I had to play. I walked out for the qualifying round, and my caddy said, "Let's go to the practice tee." There were people hitting golf balls. I did not know that people practiced golf. There were people there like Patty Berg and Betty Jameson out with their big leather shag bags and their big pile of golf balls hitting to the caddies out in the practice range. In an embarrassed tone I told my caddy, "I don't have any golf balls to hit there." I probably owned only four or five balls. He looked very disgusted and said to me, "Well, let's go to the first tee."

I played well enough that day to qualify for the championship flight. Afterwards I went home and collected 12 or 15 of my dad's old golf balls. I put them in a bag and placed them inside my golf bag. The next day I went back to the tournament.

Proudly I told my caddy, "Let's go to the practice tee." So we went down there and I pulled out of my golf bag a brown paper bag full of golf balls. I handed them to my caddy and he nearly fainted on the spot. But manfully he dumped out my little pile of balls and went out there with his brown bag and shagged my golf balls. I knew he was absolutely mortified with that bag, but I was totally green. I didn't know better. Then we went ahead and played the tournament.

I won my first match and lost my second match to Dot Kilty. From then on I wanted to be a golfer. I was hooked on it. After I became pro I received all the golf balls I could possibly want, plus fancy shag bags with my name on them and everything, like the other top pros. But you know, I probably appreciated those balls and shag bags more than anyone else in the whole LPGA.

I look back at that and laugh at myself playing with this old grocery bag and think about what must have gone through that caddy's mind.

Betsy Rawls won the Texas State Amateur four years after she took up golf. Her achievements, as the LPGA Hall of Fame will tell you, include 55 tournament wins—with four U.S. Opens, two LPGA Championships and two Western Opens to her credit. Betsy won 10 times in 1959. She is a founder of the LPGA. Betsy's Halls of Fame also include Texas, Women's Sports Foundation, and the World Golf, and she was named one of the 100 Heroes of American Golf. Betsy is currently the Executive Director for the McDonald's Kids Classic, which raises over $2,000,000 annually for charities, making it golf's greatest charity contributor.

Brooks Robinson

MY HOLE-IN-ONE

I'm not really that great of a golfer, but back in the mid-1970s I played with guys like Jim Palmer, Dave McNally and Davey Johnson. All were much better golfers than me, but I can say one thing that they can't.

At the Hillendale Country Club I hit a hole-in-one on the 14th. I never let these guys forget it. It was a pretty ugly hole-in-one, if there is such a thing. Using a seven-iron, I hit the ball about 175 yards. It bounced a few times, then rolled

25 yards across the green and went right in. Each time we play now I always ask, "Well, how many holes-in-one do you have?" That's the best part.

No, the best part was that they were all there, and we got to watch it all the way. The worst part was I still shot a 96 that day.

Hall of Famer Brooks Robinson spent his baseball career with the Baltimore Orioles. He won the coveted Golden Glove Award 16 times for his stellar performances at third base. He was a member of the 1966 and 1970 World Champion Orioles. Brooks is the expert analyst for the Orioles on radio and television.

Chi Chi Rodriguez

THE RIGHT DISCIPLINE

I don't think many people know how tough it is just to get on the tour. It may be a little easier now, although today's golfers have to go through the qualifying tournaments, called "Q school." Back in my beginning days you had to spend five years as an assistant pro before you could become an apprentice member of the PGA. Once you got that apprenticeship, you had the right to qualify (on Mondays!) in order to get into a tournament. You know I love the game of golf, I hope I

share that love everytime I walk out on a course. But you can't play competitively without hard work and discipline.

My real start as a golfer came as a kid in Puerto Rico. My parents raised us with plenty of discipline. The lights were out at 7:00 P.M. and you didn't dare challenge them by coming home late. In the mornings, we were up with the roosters, followed by a cold shower. That's all we had. Then we walked about three miles to school.

My next step towards self-discipline came in the U.S. Army. I had been a caddy when my friend Luis Guillermeti convinced me to enlist. The army made a man of me, and I found it to be one of the greatest experiences I ever had.

When I joined the tour, a guy named Pete Cooper and I teamed up. We drove to a lot of tournaments; we didn't fly much then. Quite often we'd arrive in the town of the tournament only to find no available vacancies at the hotels. So we'd sleep in the car.

I didn't have much money in those days, so when we'd pull over to a gas station and the tab came, I used to go to the bathroom. And again at restaurants when the tab came, I would get up and go to the bathroom. Finally, one day Pete said to me, "Hey, hit the hip pocket. You're gonna have to share expenses here." I don't know how I had expected to get out of it, but I sure learned my lesson then.

My first sponsors were Ed Dudley, Gene Stout and John C. Weaver. They loaned me $6,000 and that first year I made over that amount. But several years later, I found myself feeling insecure about not having any backers. So in 1965, I met with Lawrence Rockefeller. I told him I needed $12,000 a year to go on tour . . . and not only did he guarantee me that, he made me his representative of Dorado Beach. That meant I went first class everywhere, because he said, "I want you to represent us in a gentleman's way. I want you to eat in the finest restaurants and stay in the best hotels." Suddenly playing professional golf was a lot easier and a lot more fun.

My favorite golf story came when I was playing with Homero Blancas at the Masters one year. On the eighteenth hole, he hit a shot that was a little off line. It went right into the crowd; in fact, it bounced and dropped right into a lady's blouse. Well, we walked down there, and he asked, "What am I going to do?"

My sense of discipline and hard work never left me. I told him he had to play it.

Chi Chi Rodriguez was the popular winner of eight PGA Tour events and over a million dollars. Since joining the Senior Tour in 1985, he has won 20 events and three more million dollars. Chi Chi established a foundation in his name which helps abused children. He can often be found visiting a needy family or neighborhood or hospital-bound children during tournament weeks. He is a great ambassador and sportsman, helping junior golfers, and his contributions to golf are legion.

Marty Russo

PINK GYM SHOES AND GEORGE BUSH

I started playing golf only after I got out of law school and was working for a lawyer in Chicago. I noticed that he was gone every Tuesday afternoon. One day I asked him what he did on those trips out of the office. He said he went and played golf, and advised me that if I ever wanted to make it in the legal profession I should learn how to play. So, I joined Lincolnshire Country Club in Crete, Illinois as a junior member. I started with a 25 handicap and worked my way down to a 1, though now it's back to a 3.

One of my favorite golf stories happened when I was playing golf at Bermuda Dunes in a Bob Hope Desert Classic. My pro partner was Hal Sutton, who had a caddy named Gino. I hit a drive off the tee, a par-four hole, and the ball hit one of the trees on the left side of the hole. I decided I'd just punch a seven-iron to keep it under the tree line. Since I got a shot on the hole I figured I could afford to play it pretty safe. I hit it sloppily—a skull—and my fingers went numb from the mishit and jarring of the shaft. It was a worm-burner all the way up to the front edge of the green. It should have never gotten there in the first place. I had about a 75-foot uphill putt over a ridge with a four to five foot break. After looking at the shot as if I know what I'm doing, I finally ask, "Gino, what do you think I should do? I'd like to get it close, and make par for a net birdie."

He said, "Do you see that lady's foot over there? Do you see her pink gym shoes? You putt at her right foot and it will go right in."

I said, "Fine. I can't see that far, but what the heck. I'll be lucky if I get it in the same neighborhood."

Just as I was about to putt, the woman started to move. "I shouted at the top of my lungs, "Hey, lady with the pink gym shoes, DON'T MOVE!" Seventy-five feet away she stopped, pink gym shoes frozen in mid-air, and I made the shot.

We finished second runner-up in the Bob Hope tournament, thanks to a woman with an unusual taste in footwear and good hearing.

Another story I can't resist telling: One day after a meeting I received a phone call from President George Bush. He said, "I hear you've been complaining that you haven't seen me for a while." I said "I was just telling my buddies that you haven't invited me to the White House lately." He said he was setting up a golf game for Friday and asked if I wanted to join. I told the President that I had just canceled everything I had scheduled that Friday to be with him.

I showed up at the White House to find out that the others in the foursome were Dan Jenkins and Walter Payton. President Bush and I became partners—and if there's one thing I know it's that the President does not like to lose. I don't like to lose either, but he is really competitive in everything.

On the front side, I'm one under par going into the par-five ninth hole. I hit my third about 45 feet from the hole. The President's ball is near mine on the green. He got the handicap shot on that hole. Walter Payton had just finished the hole, making five for a net four. That meant the President needed to one-putt to tie the hole and halve the front nine. I said, "Why don't you putt first? Give it a go. If it goes too far don't worry, I can putt from here. We're almost on the same line so you just make sure you get it near the hole."

He hit the ball up a hill ridge with a three-foot break and it's turning up toward the hole. I said, "Mr. President, you made the putt! You made the putt!" The putt goes right in the hole, but it spins out.

CNN is taping all of this. He turned to me and said,

"You gotta make yours because I don't want to lose to these guys."

I said, "Mr. President, this is a 45-foot putt. Do you think I'm a miracle man?"

He said, "You just put it in the hole."

I answered, "Yes Sir. My Commander in Chief has spoken." I knocked it right in the center of the cup.

We tied them in the front side, rolled everything over to the back side, and I shot 68 for the day, four under par. We won our dollar bet.

Congressman Marty Russo is one of the best all-around athletes in Congress. He is a senior member of the powerful House Ways and Means Committee and a leader in Congress on health care reform and tax fairness.

Russo, who represents the Third District of Illinois, is married with two sons, one of whom, Tony, is trying to become a professional golfer.

Gene Sarazen

HER BEST SCORE EVER

United States Golf Association

In 1927 I was playing in the British Open. I received a telegram from the American ambassador, asking me if I would come to Rome and have lunch with Mussolini. I wired back and accepted.

After the Open, I asked Johnny Farrell if he would like to go to Rome with me and meet Mussolini. He said yes.

We boarded a boat that took us across the Channel, and arrived in Paris. There we boarded the Blue Train and arrived in Rome the next morning. As we approached the station, I said to Farrell, "They sure know Sarazen around here. Look out and see the red carpet they've laid out for me."

We headed for the gate and four or five embassy people met us. I thanked them for the red carpet. They said it was being rolled up. The Pope had just left for his country home.

My funniest golf story came when I was playing in the U.S. Open Championship years ago at the Oakmont Country Club and I lost by one stroke. In those days you couldn't fly, you had to go home by train. When I arrived at Pennsylvania Station in New York City, my wife met me and didn't ask how I did. Instead, she said, "Guess what I just did! I just shot an 84. My best score ever!"

I said, "What do you think I did? I lost the Open by one stroke."

Okay, I didn't think it was so funny at the time.

Gene Sarazen, known as "The Squire," won 38 professional tournaments. Among these, Gene won seven major championships, including all four majors.

Charles M. Schulz

CELEBRITIES I HAVE KNOWN

Roddy McDowall

When I was 15, I played my first round of golf—having always wanted to—and immediately fell in love with the game. Of course, the game has inspired me with a lot of golf cartoons. Since then I have drawn golf cartoons for the Crosby and AT&T National Pro-Am tournament programs for almost 35 years. I think I could draw them forever. There's just something about being out on the course that always inspires funny things. I think one of my favorites, which I drew sometime last year, shows Charlie Brown sitting on the first tee and he's reading something while Snoopy is about to tee off. Charlie Brown reads from the article, "There are now probably 21,000,000 people playing golf in our country." Snoopy looks out and says, "Yes, and they're all in the group ahead of me."

Another one I thought of recently, while playing at the AT&T National Pro-am, happened when the greens were hard to read. My caddy and I were trying to figure out which way the putt went. I said something like, "This is a hard green to read. Maybe I should wait until it comes out in paperback."

I enjoy creating certain phrases. We all know how Lee Trevino has come up with some wonderful sayings, but I've come up with one that I'm very proud of. It became the title of a golf book that I did. It's called *An Educated Slice.* I came up with the phrase because I always had a tendency to fade the ball. "I have an educated slice, but unfortunately, it only went to the first grade."

An odd occurrence happened to my friend, Jim Cummings, who died recently. He and I grew up caddying together in Minnesota and actually had to play against each other one time in the caddy championship. He's the only person that I have ever know who actually hit an airplane with a golf ball. During the war, he was stationed at an air corps base and there was a bomber taking off just a few feet from the fairway, and he hit the bomber right on the side of the fuselage.

I have always loved golf, baseball, and most other sports

stories. But I heard one recently that I think is one of my all-time favorites. I was at a golf clinic directed by Johnny Miller and someone in the crowd asked, "How do you put backspin on the golf shot?" Miller said, "I always liked the story that Sam Snead tells where someone asked how in the world he could make a golf ball have backspin. 'How do you make a ball come backwards?' And Sam said, 'About how far do you normally hit the ball?' The guy said, 'Well, I guess I hit a four iron about 130 yards.' Sam said, 'You can only hit the ball 130 yards? Why do you want it to come backwards?' " I think Sam Snead has a wonderful way of telling stories. He's one of the best there ever was at that sort of thing.

Several months ago, I was playing with a friend, and we had a dollar bet going. I was one stroke ahead of him as we came to the last fairway on the 18th. He was teeing up the ball. We always enjoy teasing each other (which happens in competitive golf). Anyway, I figured to protect my one-stroke lead, I would say something. Larry has a tendency to hook the ball, so just as he was about to tee off, I said, "Larry, did you ever notice that during this time of year the sun glints off those white, shiny, out-of-bounds stakes that run down the left side of the fairway?"

He looked up at me with disgust. And then gave his ball a good lash. He kept the ball in play, but I still won the hole—and the dollar.

I have two anecdotes that I call my conversations with famous athletes.

When I was 18 years old, I was playing in the St. Paul Open—back in the days when I tried to play in a few tournaments—and my hero was Sam Snead. I would have given anything in the world to have talked with him, just to meet him and carry on a little conversation. I finally got to talk to Sam Snead one day when I was standing near the tenth fairway. In those days they had no practice fairways at the Keller golf course in St. Paul, so we used to hit the balls out to our caddies who stood there with a shag bag. I had just finished hitting, when I heard this rumbling behind me. I turned around and there came about 100 people being led by Sam Snead right up to where I was standing. He came up to me and said, "Are you through here?" And I said, "Yes." That was my conversation with Sam Snead.

Ten years later, I was playing a practice round for the Bing Crosby Tournament. I got paired with Billy Casper—another one of my heroes. I kept trying to think of something that could start a conversation with him, and along about the third hole, nobody had really said very much up to that point. It had been raining quite hard the day before, and the fairways were still very soggy. As I was walking down the fairway, I kept thinking of some way to start a conversation with Billy. So finally I said, "Billy, when we're playing on fairways that are a little bit wet like this, do you position the ball any differently?" He said, "No." And that was my conversation with Billy Casper.

Charles "Sparky" Schulz sold his first cartoon to the *Saturday Evening Post,* and has been drawing Charlie Brown, Snoopy, Lucy, and Linus since 1950. These 40-year-old characters and their friends appear in 2,314 newspapers all over the world read by more than 100 million people daily, and "Peanuts" is translated into more than 26 languages in 67 countries. Snoopy and Charlie Brown went to the moon as mascots of the Apollo 10 astronauts in 1969. Inducted into the Cartoonists Hall of Fame in 1987, Charles has twice won comic art's highest honor, the Reuben Award. In 1990, France named him Commander of the Order of Arts and Letters for excellence in the arts. Author of hundreds of books with the "Peanuts" characters, Sparky lives in northern California with his wife, Jeannie, and is passionate about golf, ice skating, tennis, and hockey.

Patty Shehan

THE BIG BUSH

Scott Thomas

My favorite golf story took place in 1985 during the World Championship of Women's Golf in Pine Isle, Georgia. During the final round, I was leading by two shots.

On the 16th, I had hit the ball way right up on the side of a hill, and it landed smack at the base of a bush about three feet in circumferance and about two feet high. I took quite a long time trying to figure out how to hit it. I couldn't hit it from my standard right-handed stance and for a while I considered hitting it left-handed. But that wasn't a real secure shot for me either. After several minutes of stepping over the bush, around the bush, and through the bush, while trying not to break any branches or rules, I finally just stood over the bush to hit the ball. There were no stickers on it, thank God. I just took a wider stance than normal and hit it while really off balance.

Marlene Floyd was doing the commentary on the course along with Jay Randolph and Joanne Carner from the booth. While I set up, the TV camera was angled right behind me. Of course, I was wearing shorts. As I was figuring out how to hit the shot, Marlene said on nationwide television, "Patty has this big bush right between her legs."

Needless to say, every engineer back at the television trailer was rolling on the floor.

I actually didn't find out about what Marlene had said until later, when somebody came up to me and said, "Hey, Patty, how's that bush between your legs?" I just died with embarrassment.

That joke lasted for another couple of months. However, it didn't take long to learn the right protocol for everyone's derogatory questions by simply saying, "It's fine."

About the shot: despite everything, the ball went perfectly down the hill, through a few trees, and back on the fairway. Unfortunately, I lost in a play-off to Amy Alcott.

Patty Sheehan is a gifted athlete who chose to concentrate on golf. A top junior skier as a teen, Patty's natural swing has produced a dominant amateur and collegiate record and 26 LPGA wins, including two majors, in a still-active professional career. She has won over three million dollars in prize money. Some of that was used to start and fund a home for needy teen-aged females. Patty has been named *Sports Illustrated*'s "Athlete of the Year" and received numerous other awards for her contributions to society. She's a member of the Collegiate Golf Hall of Fame.

Alan Shepard

THE LUNAR GOLF SHOT

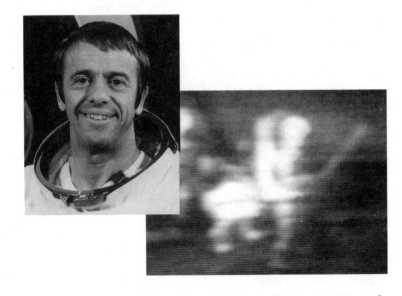

Have you ever thought about hitting a driver 1500 yards or a six-iron 900 yards? Or watching a white ball against a black sky with a time of flight of 25 to 30 seconds? What golfer even dares dream of these things?

I thought about these things during Apollo 14 in 1971. You see, the moon has one-sixth gravity of Earth. That means with the same clubhead speed, the ball will go six times as far and stay in the air (or in this case the vacuum) six times as long!

Actually, Bob Hope gave me the idea of playing golf on the moon, although he didn't know about it until months after the flight. He was visiting NASA one day—Deke Slayton and I were showing him around—and he had an old driver that he was swinging as we walked around the campus. We hooked him up in a moon walker and as he was bouncing up and down on his toes, he used the driver for balance! That's when I said, only to myself, I had to find a way to hit a ball on the moon.

Perhaps people on earth watching me on television thought it was spontaneous and unauthorized, but it was well rehearsed and all *approved* before we launched.

I had planned to use a collapsible aluminum handle, which we normally used to scoop up dust samples, since we really couldn't bend over in a pressurized suit. And then I had a golf pro design a clubhead to snap on the handle, replacing the small scoop. It was a number six iron since the handle was about as long a normal six-iron shaft. I planned to take the clubhead and two ordinary golf balls in my suit pocket—at no expense to the taxpayers!

I practiced before the flight several times in the suit-training room to be sure I could swing safely. The pressurized suit is cumbersome and I couldn't get both hands on the club; still I could make a half swing with one hand. And, finally, I checked with the "boss" and told him my plan to hit two golf balls at the very end of the lunar stay, *only* if everything went perfectly up to that point. He agreed.

Fortunately, although we had some problems earlier,

everything went just right while we were on the surface. Consequently, just before climbing up the ladder to come home, I prepared to tee off! When I dropped the first ball, it took about three seconds to land, and bounced a couple of times in the gray dust. Then, I improved my lie of course (winter rules in February) and made my best slow-motion, one-handed half-swing. Making a full swing in a space suit is impossible. I made good contact and the ball, which would have gone 30–40 yards on earth, went over 200 yards. The ball stayed up in the black sky almost 30 seconds. I was so excited I swung harder on the second one, which I shanked about 40 yards into a nearby crater! I decided to call that a hole-in-one, even if the hole was several miles in diameter.

So I folded up the golf club and climbed up the ladder to take off. The two golf balls are still there and ready to be reclaimed and reused—after all, they were new. But the club resides in a place of honor at the U.S. Golf Association in Far Hills, New Jersey, where all who see it can imagine, as did I, what a 1500-yard tee shot would really be like!

Alan Shepard was the first American launched in space, in 1961. Ten years later, he commanded Apollo 14 and became the fifth man to walk on the moon—and the first to play golf there.

Dinah Shore

GUCK

I've played in wind and rain and snow (President Ford's tournament in Vail, Colorado). I've played at the tail end of tornadoes (Furman College fundraiser). I've played in incredible sandstorms that not only pitted your car, windshield, and skin, but also blew over stately, ancient palms and ripped roofs off of houses. But one of the dumbest things I've ever done was on the fifth hole on the "Old Course" at Mission Hills. This was during the pro-am of our Nabisco Dinah Shore tournament a few years back.

The fifth is a par three, about 160 yards. Our team was not in great shape. On this hole everyone else had played shots that yielded "not-a-chance" lies. I was the last to play and since I got a handicap stroke on the hole, I had a remote chance to help our score.

I hit my ball really well. It landed on the green and as we were cheering, it took a big bounce and went into the water over the green.

We all walked to my ball. We could see that little thing floating in the "guck" just beyond the hole. Everyone was sweet about it. Don't worry's all over the place.

I had watched some tournament on television a few days earlier and seen Jack Nicklaus in a similar situation take off his shoe and sock and blast it out of the stuff. Oh, the innocence of a new, inexperienced enthusiast. I had no idea that it was impossible.

Just as Jack had done, I took off my shoes and socks and my team stared at me in utter amazement. I asked, "Do you hit down or up on it to blast out?" Somebody answered and I did whatever they said. It flew out of the water, a few remarkable feet from the hole!

I was covered with water, mud, and whatever else there is in the scum around those duck-filled ponds. I didn't care at the moment, but people gave me a wide berth all day and I guess some thought I went around that way all the time.

Incidentally, I made the putt for par, net score—a birdie! Need I tell you, I've never done it again.

Dinah Shore has a ton of talent as a singer, stage performer, and television show host, but one of her greatest achievements is being named an honorary member of the LPGA. Since 1972 her work and commitment to her special tournament, the Nabisco Dinah Shore, held in Rancho Mirage each spring, has resulted in every LPGA player calling her "friend."

George P. Shultz

A HOLE-IN-ONE NOT TO BE PROUD OF

Stanford University's Visual Art Services

My most disheartening golf story is about my only hole-in-one. The fifth hole at the Orchards in South Hadley, Massachusetts is a 160-yard par three. You can see the green from the tee.

On this day I half skulled my drive. It hit the lip of the trap in front of the green, bounced up, and rolled into the cup.

I claimed the hole-in-one but with little satisfaction, let alone exhilaration.

George P. Schultz has had multi-faceted careers in academia, business and government. For eight years he was President and a Director of Bechtel Group. He served President Nixon as Secretary of Labor, Director of the Office of Management and Budget, and Secretary of the Treasury. From 1982 to 1989 he served as U.S. Secretary of State. He currently teaches at Stanford University and is a Distinguished Fellow at the Hoover Institution.

19 Tommy Smothers

MY WIFE, MY LOVER, MY CADDY

My wife Marcy and I share a passionate love for the game of golf. As I was preparing for the AT&T National Pro-am, Marcy decided she wanted to be my caddy. She knows my swing well, and I felt her temperate disposition would be an asset under the pressure of competition.

On the first morning of the tournament, I met my golf instructor, John Redman, on the practice tee. I hit my pitching wedge first, working to find my tempo. Redman suggested that I take a full swing with my seven-iron. I topped my first three shots. Maybe my nerves were already affecting me.

Redman told me to slow down and shorten my back-swing. The next three shots were topped *and* thin. I heard hysterical laughter behind me. I recognized that voice. It was my wife—my *caddy*—laughing at me.

Just the day before, I had played the round of my life: I shot a 78 in a practice round at Pebble Beach! Now, just minutes from the first tee, my caddy was ridiculing my swing. I make my living as a comedian, but I've never been laughed at this way before!

We made our way to the starter's tent. Marcy handed me my driver as my name was announced. I would be the first to hit in my group. The gallery was hushed. The birds were singing. I had quieted all of the golfers in my mind, and reminded myself of the *27 Most Important Things to Remember at the Moment of Impact.* * Then I heard deep, deep breathing. I looked up to see my caddy doing Lamaze-like breaths in an effort to calm me. Where had she learned this technique? Certainly not in the PGA caddy seminar she attended at the Santa Rosa Open. I gave her a look that was more irate husband than disgruntled player, and she backed off knowingly.

I took my stance and hit my inaugural drive long but left into the rough. Not bad for the first tee, and my caddy thankfully gave me an approving smile.

It was a beautiful day at Pebble Beach, but I wasn't able to come close to my personal best. Nevertheless, with the help of my handicap, I got the team to six under.

Our second round began on the tenth tee at Spyglass Hill. We were feeling confident the team might be able to get to 15 under that day. I was striking the ball better, but my performance on the greens left something to be desired.

*Book by T.S. on golf

The group behind us included co-leader Jeff Sluman, and we were forever hearing the gallery roar for the eagle and birdie putts that he was sinking hole after hole. After yet another ovation on the thirteenth green, it was with a combination of dashed hope and disgust that my caddy handed me my putter on 14 and said, "See if you can make this one, Buster."

I didn't, and we remained 8 under, 10 under total for two rounds. We walked somewhat dejectedly from the 18th to the courtesy transportation. The driver opened the trunk of the van and asked us how our day went. I started to mutter something, when my caddy broke in with, "You know, Tom, if I really wanted to make it worth my while to carry a 30-pound bag for miles a day, I should have carried Sluman's bag!"

Another day at the office with my wife, my lover, my caddy.

Our final round on Saturday was at Poppy Hills, and I was relieved not to be on the network television rotation this year. I was looking forward to small galleries and a casual pace. I never expected Marcy to start "playing" the crowds, but she did. We had an improbable gallery of 50 or so spectators. We were the last group off the tee and the stragglers followed us in.

On the twelfth hole that day, the 48th of the tournament, my short drive left me 230 yards uphill to the pin. Roger Maltbie and his group were ahead of us on the green. Marcy handed me a three-wood. I asked our pro to confirm the distance. He said, "Hit it with everything you've got. You'll never make it there." I turned to my caddy, and asked for Big Bertha. I rarely hit my driver off the fairway, but it was my only chance to get close. With a frustrated and drawn look, she replaced the three-wood and slapped Bertha into my hand and demanded, "You better hit it, Bucko!"

With only six holes to go, we were 14 under, and I got a stroke on this hole. A well-placed shot could give us a chance at a net eagle and put us in contention for making the cut. I approached the ball, waggled twice, and made the best move I've made in years. The ball went sailing low and straight to the pin. I looked up and it was still sailing straight, past 200 yards, and was headed towards Maltbie on the green. It plugged just a yard short of the green in the rough, ten yards below the pin.

Not only had "Bucko" hit it, but I had hit it too well. Now I had to fear Maltbie's wrath. The gallery clapped in delight, my caddy was *shocked,* and I hung my head low, knowing I had inadvertently violated a basic rule of golf etiquette.

When our group reached the cleared green, the marshals informed me that Maltbie was standing over his putt when my ball landed. I was relieved to hear that he laughed when he heard it was Smothers' ball—and that he had been able to regroup and sink the putt.

Unfortunately, my composure was not easily regained. I chili-dipped my chip and three-putted for a bogey net par. We finished at 14 under, which was not only respectable but a tremendous improvement over the year before, when my team was 13 over.

In just two years of playing at the AT&T, I had bettered my score by 27 strokes. Maybe it was luck. Perhaps a year of hard work and practice had paid off. Certainly it was my patience. But I still like to attribute part of my success to my wife, my lover, my caddy.

The guitar-playing **Tommy Smothers** and his bass-playing brother Dick have been entertaining people for over 30 years. They have had their own prime-time comedy series in the 1960s and the 1980s, have headlined in Las Vegas, appeared on numerous television programs and talk shows, and earned a retrospective and seminar on their work at the Museum of Broadcasting in New York City. Tom is the only golfer known who can sink a putt using a yo-yo. Only the most dedicated yo-ing golfer can appreciate such prowess.

Sam Snead

MY SECRET WEAPON

Golfers in love do foolish things!

We have all heard about or watched the way newlyweds walk into walls, or drop the ring. Early in my career I was prone to these types of incidents too, but they let me discover my secret weapon in golf.

I got married on August 15, 1939, I think! We spent our first night in Cumberland, Maryland, on our way to Niagara Falls for the honeymoon. Believe me, I remember all of the honey, but I don't remember seeing any moon that night. We got up at eight in the morning and set out to drive to Buffalo and then on to Niagara Falls. We were on Route 219 when we came to a detour.

Let me remind you, I was a man in love, given to sudden losses of concentration. I took a turn where I thought the arrow pointed us, and drove through some beautiful territory. At four o'clock in the afternoon, though, I began to suspect that we weren't exactly where we wanted to be. I stopped to ask, and was told to go back to Cumberland and pick up Route 219! We had driven almost the entire day in the wrong direction.

We had to hurry on to Niagara Falls, because I was due in Toronto a few days later to compete in the Canadian Open. I allowed myself to fantasize how wonderful it would be to win the tournament while on my honeymoon—but made sure there would be no repeating lovers' mistakes while on the road.

As it turned out, my next lovers' error was discovered on the first tee. Bobby Cruikshank and Denny Shute were watching as I stepped out with one golf shoe on and one street shoe. Shute spoke out very loudly, "Boy, Sam will probably lose 15 yards at least."

I hurried back to the clubhouse and changed the shoe. I raced to the first tee and my shot went beautifully. Dismayed, Bobby said, "Yuk! He just added a bloody 25 yards!!"

Despite the lovers' goofs, I won the tournament. I really think my secret weapon was being in love.

Legendary and smooth-swinging **Sam Snead** won 81 PGA Tour events between 1937 and 1965. He won three PGA Championships, one British Open, three Masters, served on eight Ryder Cups teams and six World Cup teams, was leading money winner three times, and won the Vardon Trophy for lowest scoring average four times. Sam is a member of the PGA and World Golf Halls of Fame.

Jan Stephenson

MASH NOTES

Dick Zimmerman

Pro golfers love their fans, but women pros especially have to beware sometimes. One of my fans caught my notice by writing to me all the time. He claimed to be in love with me. He used to write in italic script: beautiful italic calligraphy. He'd write these beautiful poems that were really too long. After a while, I stopped reading them because he clearly wasn't all there—saying he loved me though he didn't even know me. Still, I knew he kept writing me because he had that special handwriting and everyone wanted to look at his letters.

After people pestered me, I finally said, "Here!" and handed over the latest letter. Everybody in the locker room just loved to see them. Every week I would get this envelope and my friends would tell me about the lovely poem inside saying how wonderful I was. He used to rhyme about my putts or what he'd seen on television.

One letter announced he was going to show up at a tournament I was playing. I alerted the event director.

Sure enough, as I was putting someone suddenly called out. I was in the middle of the tournament and he called out, "Jan! I'm your love that has been writing. If you recognize me, I have the keys to a Mercedes right here. If you recognize that I'm your love, then you can have this car." Everybody turned around and somebody in the gallery said, "Take that car!"

We had him taken off the course. An hour later he was back, dressed in a tennis outfit. The director had him escorted off. The next day I got a letter in the familiar penmanship that said, "I'll be there Sunday. When you finish we'll get married."

I was a little nervous but I knew that the tournament officials would do whatever was necessary to protect me. All the other players loved it. They couldn't wait until Sunday to see if he'd show up. So sure enough, I was on the fifth hole and lining up my putt. I looked up and there he was—standing there waiting for me dressed in a white suit and holding a bouquet. All the girls couldn't wait. They were all saying, "We saw him! We saw him!"

He was escorted from the course again. None of us have heard from him again, unless he has changed his writing style.

Jan Stephenson hails from New South Wales, Australia. She now lives in the U.S. full-time, and is still active in her career. She has earned victories in 16 events on the LPGA Tour, including three majors. Exercise videos, golf course design, and a line of golf clubs and bags for a major manufacturer are some of her off-the-course business interests.

Curtis Strange
THE ONES THAT GOT AWAY

Lawrence Levi

In the late 1970s, when I was pretty new to the PGA Tour, I was playing with Chi Chi Rodriguez. We got to the ninth hole, which was our 36th, and were crossing a bridge over a canal. I don't know what caused my caddy to lose his balance but suddenly he was falling into the canal, about 10 feet below. I grabbed him by the arm, another fellow grabbed him by the neck, or something. Slowly we tried to hoist him up, but neither of us had a good grip. As we lifted him, we

watched the clubs—one by one—go into the water. Everything I had was gone except my putter, two-iron, four-iron,
and five-iron. Luckily, I could play the last hole with the
two-iron and five-iron. I think that this was some of the most
pressure I've ever been under. I knew that if I missed the
green I wouldn't have any club to use to get the ball out of
a bunker.

As I walked on the side of the fairway I met up with Jack
Tuthill, the Tour rules official. He was up on the right just
laughing like hell at me. He later explained that I could have
replaced all the clubs if I needed to. But I made par on the
hole. Somebody dove into the canal and found half the clubs.
We had a diver come out the next day and find all the rest of
the clubs right before I teed off. It was so embarrassing.

Everybody had such a good time with it, but you know
the locker rooms—they're brutal. If you don't have thick skin
to walk through the men's locker rooms, and I'm sure even
the women's locker rooms, you can't make it.

Here's another story: I just finished number one on the
money list in 1985. The first tournament in 1986 was Tucson,
Arizona. In the Wednesday pro-am, I was announced to the
first tee while thinking, "I'm pretty sporty, now. I'm pretty
good."

On my way I went to jump the the gallery rope and I
tripped and fell flat on my face. I didn't think that anybody
noticed because I got up so quick. Inside I'm thinking, "Yeah,
uh huh."

I get announced. I'm not really listening, but I catch, "Here's the 1985 leading money winner, Arnold Palmer Award winner . . . whatever, whatever, whatever . . . blah, blah, blah . . . and former high jump champion in the 1984 Olympics. . . ."

It was very strange. I tried to smile and act like this happened all the time, but people were falling down laughing. I'll tell you what, I couldn't even get it off the tee.

Clearly my biggest disappointment was losing the 1985 Masters. I like talking about it though. Every time you go back and relive it is good therapy.

When I lost, it just so happened that that's the biggest lead I ever lost. It just so happened to be in a major. True, after the first round, all I hoped for was just to make sure I made the cut. Surprise! On Sunday I had a four-shot lead, with nine to go.

By losing I learned how much that hurt. I literally didn't sleep; I dreamt or nightmared, and just never stopped thinking about it, until I played golf again, which was two weeks later.

I like to think it was good that I lost. If I hadn't, maybe I would not have won two Opens after that. What I mean is, I knew I was not going to get a lead and lose again. I think you learn and you remember and you just remember that feeling. So, you try that much harder when you get a lead in a big tournament. You don't want to go through the pain again. You put in that little extra effort and dig a little deeper. Sometimes you win on just pure guts. It's as simple as that.

As for learning things, you take the bad with the good. That was a tough time. People don't realize. People always look on Sunday afternoon at the winners waving to the crowd and getting the trophy and the check. And they forget about the guy who worked just as hard to get a check for $2,000 to finish last. They don't see Curtis Strange that night after losing a four-shot lead.

I've talked a lot about how to win, being a winner, and about things like that with a friend of mine, Mr. Arnold Palmer. He's always saying, "Win graciously!" That was his main thing and I think that's the theme of our conversations throughout the years. But I think you've also got to lose with some class, too. I think that was the most important time I had to suck it up and lose with some class—because the world was looking at me. Thankfully, people have a lot of compassion and sympathy when something like that happens.

Later that year I beat Nicklaus and Norman head-to-head at the Canadian Open. That helped me get over being known as one of the guys who blew a big lead at the Masters. Since then I've not played well at the Masters. I've wanted to play well there, too hard, and I end up playing badly.

When somebody says, "What tournament do you want to win, if you had one tournament left to win?" Well, the answer with my heart would be the Masters. But if I answered with my brain, it would be my third U.S. Open.

Curtis Strange had a strong amateur and collegiate career. As a pro, Curtis has stepped into the victory circle 17 times so far. Two of the biggest were back-to-back U.S. Open titles in 1988 and 1989. The leading money winner in 1985, 1987, and 1988, he has represented the U.S. in Ryder Cup play four times. Strange was named PGA Player of the Year in 1988.

19 Louise Suggs

MAKING THE UNMAKEABLE

I started playing golf when my father built a nine-hole public golf course outside of Atlanta in Lithia Springs. We moved there in 1933 and lived on the golf course. I started playing when I was about ten years old. I'd pick up golf clubs with wooden shafts and my father would saw them off and make grips out of bicycle tape. I guarantee if you tried to put your hands on a club with that tape on it, you'd never turn it loose.

Most of the caddies on the golf course were my school-mates and we would play a game we called "short knocker." There might be fifteen to twenty of us hitting golf balls off the first tee and the shortest knocker had to go pick them all up. I tried not to be the short knocker by just hitting the ball as hard and as far as I could.

The golf course was built during the depression and everybody thought Dad was nuts. And I guess he was, sort of. But there was no public golf course around Atlanta, so it turned out well. The fees were fifty cents for 18 holes during the week and seventy-five cents on the weekend. When he went up to seventy-five cents and one dollar, everybody raised Cain and threatened never to come back.

My dad's coaching was mostly spiritual I'd say. His advice was along the lines of, "Do what you have to do. If you think you're supposed to hit an eight-iron, but you don't want to use an eight-iron, try something else. Just do the job the best way you can." He'd been a professional ballplayer, a pitcher, and his philosophy was, "Get the ball over the plate. I don't care how you get it over there, so long as you don't cheat. Get it over the plate."

One time, I was hitting balls and asked him, "Do you see anything radically wrong?" He said, "No, it looks all right to me." I was hitting pretty well, but sensed there was still something wrong. He asked me, "How does your grip feel?" I said, "Fine." He said, "Then it's wrong." His lesson was if anything gets too comfortable, you had better double check it because something is wrong. That was his attitude for athletic endeavors of any sort.

My most embarrassing moment came in White Plains, at the beginning of my professional career. I was staying at the old Roger Smith Hotel. There was no air conditioning in those days and I suffered from bad allergies. They would get so bad my tongue would stick to the roof of my mouth and all I could do was chew ice and try to get some air into my lungs. At about 2:00 one morning I threw a robe over my pajamas, went downstairs, and told the desk clerk that I was going outside to see if I could get my sinuses to open up. The hotel was on the corner and had a marquis on the front. While I walked around trying to breathe, I notice this policeman inching closer and closer to me. He finally stopped me and said, "What are you doing out here?" I tried to explain, but my purse was back in the room, and I had no identification with me. I told him to check with the desk clerk if he didn't believe me, but he couldn't find the desk clerk. In the meantime, some man came up and started to talk to me. The policeman was watching all of this from the hotel lobby and that clinched it for him. He just figured I was working up a little "trade." He was about to arrest me until eventually I found the desk clerk who verified my story.

My favorite golf story: at the 1967 U.S. Women's Open at Hot Springs, Virginia, we played the Cascade's Lower Course. It was the final round and I was near the clubhouse at the fifteenth green, a par three. Byron Nelson and Chris

Schenkel were the television commentators. I could hear them broadcasting the play-by-play while I was on the green putting. I really hadn't thought too much about winning the tournament, but I knew I was in pretty good shape. I made a rather long putt for a par and I could hear Byron say, "There's no way she could have made that putt. It's not makeable from that position." So I turned around and looked up at him and yelled, "Well, it must have been makeable. I made it."

Louise Suggs has one of the sweetest swings ever in golf. A brilliant amateur career produced many wins. The most outstanding were the U.S. Amateur, the British Amateur, and two professional major titles. After turning pro and being a founding member of the LPGA, Louise won immediately and ultimately compiled a 50-win record. She is in the Georgia, World Golf, Women's Sports Foundation, and LPGA Halls of Fame. Louise is one of the 100 Heroes of American Golf.

Kathleen Sullivan

PLAYING WITH ARNOLD

It was Arnie's 60th birthday. Time for his friends to celebrate years of championship moments. And, like any occasion involving Arnold Palmer, a charity was to benefit. The Orlando Children's Hospital was throwing Arnie the party, and golf's gallery king asked me to come down and moderate the ceremonies. Quite an honor.

On Sunday morning, Arnie took me out to see his latest creation, Isleworth. We had time to play nine before brunch and jumped in the cart.

Arnie is as masterful with his short irons as he is at putting you at ease. But then you see that signature swing and realize that you have to hit next! I shanked more short shots that day than I care to remember.

What I can't forget is what happened on the fourth— or was it the fifth?—hole. Arnie was surrounded that Sunday by his personal Army, which included Isleworth's course superintendent and Arnold's partner in golf course design, Ed Seay. Arnold teed off, then it was my turn.

Standing on the ladies' tee box, I was bewildered. Dead center, 60 yards in front of me, stood a tree the size of Texas. I looked over at the master and asked, "Arnie, do I hit a wedge over it, or punch a low iron through it?"

He had no idea what I meant. So he came over to the tee area, stood there with his hands on his hips in disbelief, then looked at Ed Seay and said, "Pull it."

Arnie said he had never seen the golf course from a woman's perspective until that day. So I hit a fine drive down the middle of the fairway and then clubbed a great three-wood just short of the green. I said to the course super that it was a pretty long par four. He told me it was a five. I looked over, and Arnie was in the trees, trying to find his second shot. Kiddingly, I yelled, "Hey, Arnie, what're you hitting?" He looked back at me with a competitive fire in his eyes.

I won that hole, and took with me a lifetime memory that can't fit on any scorecard.

Kathleen Sullivan has been a national newscaster for more than 12 years. She was one of the first Americans to broadcast live from the Soviet Union in the 1970s, put CNN on the air in 1980, and was a fixture on morning television in the 1980s. In 1984, she became the first woman to anchor the Olympics for American television at the Games in Sarajevo and Los Angeles. This summer in Barcelona, Kathleen will anchor the Olympics Triplecast pay-per-view coverage. She played varsity tennis while attending USC and took up golf at the urging of one of her bridesmaids, Amy Alcott. She currently resides in New York and Rancho Mirage, where she contributes some of her energies to the Desert Aids Project.

Tom Sullivan

EGO DESTRUCTION

Chris Barr

All of my experiences in golf are my favorite golf stories.
The whole issue for me playing golf is a story in itself.
I tried tennis and I had a great serve, but if my opponents hit
it back I had a problem. So tennis was a lousy choice. I wanted
something I could share, because I had played individual
sports all of my life: wrestling, running, etc., and those things
were very isolated. So when I took up golf, I used to go to
the driving range and people would talk about me out loud
out there as if I was either deaf or dead. I'd pick up a five-iron
and a guy would say, "What do you think, Charlie? You think

he's gonna hit it?'' I got kind of pissed off about it, so I had to decide what to do.

I had this wonderful golden retriever seeing-eye dog named Dinah. When Dinah was a baby, I trained her to retrieve golf balls by pouring aftershave all over them. Then we'd go out at night, because what the hell did I care; I'd hit them and she'd go get them. It was a great process. But, like so many things in life, humans can overestimate their skills.

From my house to the Pacific Ocean is 93 yards. And from my house to the four-story apartment complex that blocks part of the view is 41 yards. I had a nine-iron and I thought, ''if I hit this sucker perfectly, I can hit it over the top of the building and into the ocean. I know I can.'' So I wound up like a coiled spring and rocketed the ball right through this guy's dining room window, probably apartment 3C. And I thought, ''What now?'' I did the only thing that made sense: I ran into my house, because I figured he'd never think a blind guy did that. He came down for me and said, ''Now Sullivan, I've read your books, and I loved you on 'Johnny Carson' and all those shows, but that window's gonna cost you $170.''

Most people are terrified of sand shots. I figured out how to play them. For ''Good Morning America,'' I had to play nine holes with Jack Nicklaus and I was supposed to interview him while we played. Well, I was panicked. It was the opening of one of Nicklaus' courses, so they had press and everybody there. We got to the first tee and the announcer said, ''Ladies and gentlemen, now on the first tee, the winner of 70 lifetime events, five-times Masters, four-times British Open, three-times U.S. Open Champion: Jack Nicklaus." Well, he hit a drive that I heard. It not only went out, but up and then out—one of those skyrockets that lasts and lasts.

Then the announcer said, "Now, ladies and gentlemen, on the tee, blind Tom Sullivan."

My knees were gone. (I'd had two Jameson's on the rocks because I was so scared.) But I hit a great shot, one of my lifetime best, right out next to Nicklaus. I was five yards behind him, so I had to hit first. I said to him, "You built this course. How far is it to the center?" He said, "Well, Tom, it's 164 yards to the front. You gotta hit a four-iron here because the wind's a little in your face." I said to him, "What would you hit?" And he said, "Well, I'd be looking at a hard seven-iron, or maybe a choked down six. I said, "Jack, I know you're a lot stronger than I am, but I don't know. I'm pretty pumped up. I don't know if I can hit this." He said, "Oh, no. You gotta hit the four." So I hit it, and I hit dead, solid perfect. And Jack said, "Great shot! It's right at the flag, only it carried into the back trap." I looked at him and said, "Too much club, Jack."

When we reached the bunker, Jack said to me, "Tom, this is really a tough shot. This is a high lip. I built this in the tradition of small bunker, high side. Why don't you just take it out and we'll go to the next tee." I said, "No, I'll take one shot at it." I made a great blast and tapped in for par. I don't think Jack will ever forget it and neither will I. The spectators applauded and cheered like crazy!

Another time, playing with Dave Stockton at the Hartford Open, my second shot on 18 was real good and landed in the trap in front of the green. We walked up to the green. Stockton came over to me and said, "Tom, please don't catch this thin. You'll kill somebody. We've got 10,000 people around this green and if you do this wrong, you'll be a dead person." That's a horrible thought to go into the bunker with.

I sunk that shot for birdie. Stockton didn't even putt. He just walked off. The people roared. I was grinning from ear to ear.

One of my special sports heroes has always been Sam Snead. In 1976, I went to play the Ed McMahon-Moline Open. Sam at that time was 67 years old and that was his last PGA event. The first day he shot a 68. The second day he shot 68. He was eight under. The third day he shot 69. So he was 11 under and two shots out of the lead. I woke up on Sunday morning. Ed McMahon had to leave and I was going to give the awards. As I was leaving the hotel, Sam was coming in. He hadn't been to bed yet. I don't know where he'd been. I have heard that he liked to party. I said, "Mr. Snead, have you already been out practicing?" He said, "Well, yeah . . . in a matter of speaking."

I said, "Mr. Snead, you've got a chance to win this tournament. Aren't you tired?" He replied, "Nope. Son, I figured that at my age, it's either going to be there, or it's not. And this was the best way I could think of to relax."

He lost the tournament by three shots—but they just don't create men like this anymore.

When I play, if I play well, people contract an interesting disease called Sullivanitis. Sullivanitis is when you stand on a tee with a strange foursome and you're playing for a Nassau bet. I purposely hit first. I crush one and the guy behind says, "Uh-oh, now I gotta hit it." He's gone for the day. He'll never play well because his ethic is built around the idea that if the blind guy can hit it, he's got to kill it.

Golf is the game that has given me a sense of balanced self-image. I have been able to share it with human beings and make my blindness less relevant than the fun of playing the game. The pleasure of playing the game, sitting in the bar afterwards talking about shots—all of those things made me feel like I belonged. On the other hand, it's such a humbling game that for a guy in show business it's probably a necessary ego destroyer. I view golf as the joy of my social process.

Tom Sullivan is an actor, singer, entertainer, producer and author. He has written two children's books, a book about his guide dog, *The Leading Lady: Dinah's Story,* and an autobiography, *If You Could See What I Hear,* which was turned into a major motion picture.

Dick Taylor

OPEN INVITATION

McKenzie Dickerson

When former Chairman David Foster involved the Colgate Palmolive Company in golf during the 1970s, his really big show was the Dinah Shore Winner's Circle championship out in the Palm Springs desert. He graciously invited me to play in the pro-am events. So I'd bring my seven-piece swing out west and he'd very kindly pair me with Sandra Obscurity with a 4:00 A.M. tee time. No sweat!

After David and I got to be friends via Colgate's sponsorship of the Hall of Fame tournament in my Pinehurst, North Carolina backyard and at the terrific Colgate European Women's Open at Sunningdale, England, things changed for me.

No longer did I get those dewy tee times with no-names. David once paired me with Bob Hope, which is *not* exactly the favor or fun one might think. Bob is there to entertain, not play golf, and David reveled in my post-round description of having my ball run over by Hope's cart, and his gallery overrun me during a backswing.

Another year found me teamed on a super team with defender Sandra Post, hostess Dinah, and the captain of Sunningdale, a proper gentleman indeed. The day started with the practice tee. Next to me was Lawrence Welk, then in his television heyday.

Lawrence tried to relax me by correctly remarking that between the two of us we sounded like a bowl of Rice Krispies as we hit practice shots. While most golfers hope to stretch muscles and tune swings, there is a level of golfers who hope only to loosen enough tendons to get the club back at the first tee.

Called to the tee, we watched Welk and friends drive, and 800 lavender-heads bobbed down the fairway after him. Our turn and Miss Post, one of my favorites on the LPGA tour, zinged off a shot, the English guy did a little handsy draw shot, then it was my turn. Dinah sauntered over to me and whispered, "Honey, your fly is open!"

My stomach flipped. My blood turned cold. Then I got

the giggles. I had been wandering around Mission Hills for
at least an hour since going to the bathroom, so no telling
what a sight I had been to behold. Then I performed the
slickest trick in my life. I bent over and teed up the ball, all
the while laughing, and as I straightened up I deftly zipped
up, all in one fluid motion. I looked around at Miss Shore.
"Nice move," she told me. Fighting off the lingering giggles
and much to my surprise, I hit a good drive. Then she topped
her shot.

Later, we agreed the funky gold golf shoes I was wearing
had detracted eyes from my open fly. It was the fiftieth anni-
versary of the Etonic shoe company and I was given the shoes
with a dare to wear them at Dinah's. She wanted to know,
"did Ruby Keeler give those to you?"

Dick Taylor has written about golf's players during
six decades. He is a three-time winner of the Golf
Writers Association's magazine division top award.
In 1991, he was honored with two new distinctions:
PGA of America's Lifetime Achievement Award in
Journalism and the Memorial Golf Journalism
Award. Dick is one of the 100 Heroes of American
Golf. Always one to keep track of that sort of thing,
this curmudgeon has covered over 620 tournaments,
including 88 majors. For 28 years he was editor of
Golf World USA Weekly magazine. Since 1990 he has
syndicated his work in five golf magazines.

Ken Venturi

BING AND I

"Bing Crosby wants you on the telephone!"

I was 20 years old, sitting in a classroom at San Jose State University, when these words were spoken in my direction.

I immediately thought this was some kind of practical joke, but could hardly ignore that the teacher had delivered the message, not a student. As I walked out of class I read two looks on the faces of my fellow students: either they accused me of being a big shot, or a fool for believing the message was real!

I made my way to the phone, thinking of what I should say to the person who had gotten me out of class on such a totally unbelievable pretext. I was ready with a zinger or two, although I started off casual.

"Hello," I said.

"Hello," the voice replied. "This is Bing Crosby."

It hit me like a two-by-four. There was no other voice like that in the world. Suddenly I was speechless. Bing Crosby at the time was one of the biggest names in show business and in golf. I wasn't in show business, so that couldn't be the reason for the call. I played golf pretty well. As a matter of fact, the previous year I had won the California State Amateur Championship. But that would hardly be enough to attract Bing Crosby's attention, right?

"Hey, Mr. Crosby, what can I do for you?"

That voice came back through the phone like a pouring of maple sugar over waffles. "Ken, I've got a problem and I need your help."

I cleared my throat. "Sure. What can I do for you?"

"One of our amateurs has dropped out and we have a pro who doesn't have an amateur and I would consider it a personal favor if you would help us out and come down and play in our tournament."

To me, this was the equivalent of a young knight getting a message from King Arthur to come to the castle and participate in the Royal Joust. I tried to answer respectfully and not let it sound like I thought I had died and gone to heaven. "I'd love to," I said. "I'll get off school and come find a place to stay." This was a Wednesday, so I knew I'd have to arrange things quickly.

"There's no place to be found. Everything's been taken," Bing replied, and my heart dropped. "You know where I live on the golf course?"

"Yes."

"You stay with me," he said.

"With you?" I said.

"You got it!" he said.

Here I am, 20 years old, and the biggest name in the world is asking me to play in his tournament and stay in his home. On the way back to class I wasn't sure whether to tell everyone the truth or that it was a wrong number. I could just hear some wise guy say, "Sure, and next week you'll be lunching with Ben Hogan."

I decided to tell the truth. And honestly, I enjoyed the reaction. Wouldn't you?

I drove through the front gate of the San Francisco city tournament—the first time I'd ever done that anywhere. I was sure that when I announced myself to the guard he would say, "Ken who?" But he didn't. I received the royal treatment. In fact, I received the Crosby treatment, which was better. When I announced that I was Ken Venturi and that I was supposed to be staying with Mr. Crosby, the guard said, "Yes, Mr. Venturi. Mr. Crosby is expecting you. Go right in." I drove in like I was driving on clouds.

In the tournament, I played with a pro named Mark Fry. We made the cut, but I can't recall how well we did.

Later, when I turned pro, I realized how long-lasting Bing's appreciation was for my coming to his rescue way back in 1950. I always got to pick my own partner in the Crosby Tournament. Bing always said, "Ken, whatever you want to do." In fact, the year that I won the tournament, I was the last one off the tee. The wind was blowing and it was raining hard, and Bing said, "Ken do you want to call it?" And I said, "Nah. They're all out there. We might as well go with it. What's the difference?" I was leading by two shots and finished with a 77. I won by three.

As the Crosby Clambake was an official event, I got an invitation from Bing my first year as a pro, 1957. I heard some grumbling from other pros who didn't like the idea that I got a direct invitation and they had to qualify. So I went to Bing and told him that I had to qualify too. Bing said I had the invite if I wanted it, but I told him I wanted to qualify because I had to play with these guys all my life and I didn't want them saying I got special treatment. I went out to Pebble Beach and shot 69. I made the tournament.

I look back on that phone call as one of the great joys of my life. And my relationship with Bing turned into a lifetime of pleasure. I'm sure there are many other people who have felt the same way about him.

Ken Venturi won 14 events on the PGA Tour. In 1964, he won the U.S. Open in dramatic fashion and high heat at the Congressional Country Club and was named PGA Player of the Year. Ken served as a Ryder Cup playing member in 1965. He has been the color commentator for CBS's golf telecasts for 25 years. Ken is also a golf course design consultant.

Helen Sigel Wilson

THE MOST CONSIDERATE GOLFER IN THE WORLD

Bachrach

I was playing in the finals of the Philadelphia City Championship one year. My opponent was my nemesis, Dorothy Porter. We had about 150 or so in the gallery. I was probably 34 years old. That was about two years ago. [Just kidding.]

I was playing in the finals and I had a young boy caddying for me. We came to the eleventh hole, which is a par three. I teed the ball up and then I felt some big rain drops. I said to my caddy, "It's beginning to rain. We better get my rain jacket out of the golf bag." While he was getting it out I teed my ball up and hit my shot, and watched it land. Then I turned to get my jacket and the caddy was zipping it up—on himself!

Anyway, he wore it. Some of my friends were there and they were dying laughing. He wore it the rest of the round and wimpy me got soaked. I never said a word to him about it. I didn't have enough nerve. All I can say is he must have thought that I was the most considerate golfer in the world.

I did win. Otherwise I probably would have hit him on the head and ripped the jacket off of him. You know I can be a very poor sport.

Helen Sigel Wilson won the Eastern Amateur three times, the Western Amateur in 1949, Pennsylvania State five times, the Philadelphia City 14 times, two Curtis Cup teams, and for the "thrill of her life" was named Captain of the Curtis Cup team in 1978. She was a very long ball hitter, at only 5'4" and 130 pounds. Helen is an executive with Diversified Search, Inc. in Philadelphia, where she specializes in management recruiting for country clubs.

Henny Youngman

ONE-LINERS

I played Civil War golf. I went out in 61 and came back in 65.

I play golf to relax, when I'm too tired to mow the lawn.

You play golf with your own worst enemy—yourself.

Henny Youngman can tell 200–250 jokes in 45 minutes. He recently appeared in the movie "Goodfellas" and wrote his autobiography, *Take My Life, Please!*